# Dr. Scudder's

Tales for Little Readers,

About the Heathen.

Dr. John Scudder

**Alpha Editions**

This edition published in 2021

ISBN : 9789355346513

Design and Setting By
**Alpha Editions**
www.alphaedis.com
Email - info@alphaedis.com

As per information held with us this book is in Public Domain. This book is a reproduction of an important historical work. Alpha Editions uses the best technology to reproduce historical work in the same manner it was first published to preserve its original nature. Any marks or number seen are left intentionally to preserve its true form.

# Contents

CHAPTER I. — 1 —

GENERAL REMARKS — 1 —

CHAPTER II. — 3 —

THE COLOR AND ORNAMENTS OF THE HINDOOS. — 3 —

CHAPTER III. — 8 —

DRESS, HOUSES, EATING, AND SALUTATION OF THE HINDOOS. — 8 —

CHAPTER IV. — 13 —

MARRIAGE AMONG THE HINDOOS. — 13 —

CHAPTER V. — 16 —

DEATH AND FUNERALS OF THE HINDOOS. — 16 —

CHAPTER VI. — 19 —

THE GODS OF THE HINDOOS. — 19 —

CHAPTER VII. — 21 —

THE THREE HUNDRED AND THIRTY MILLIONS OF THE GODS OF THE HINDOOS—THE CREATION OF THE UNIVERSE—THE TRANSMIGRATION OF SOULS—THE DIFFERENT HELLS. — 21 —

| | |
|---|---|
| CHAPTER VIII. | - 25 - |
| HINDOO CASTES. | - 25 - |
| CHAPTER IX. | - 29 - |
| HINDOO TEMPLES—CARS—PROCESSION OF IDOLS. | - 29 - |
| CHAPTER X. | - 35 - |
| FESTIVALS OF THE HINDOOS. | - 35 - |
| CHAPTER XI. | - 38 - |
| THE WORSHIP OF THE SERPENT. | - 38 - |
| CHAPTER XII. | - 40 - |
| THE RIVER GANGES. | - 40 - |
| CHAPTER XIII. | - 45 - |
| THE GODDESS DURGA. | - 45 - |
| CHAPTER XIV. | - 49 - |
| THE GODDESS KARLE. | - 49 - |
| CHAPTER XV. | - 54 - |
| SELF-TORTURES OF THE HINDOOS. | - 54 - |
| CHAPTER XVI. | - 62 - |
| THE SUTTEE, OR BURNING OF WIDOWS. | - 62 - |
| CHAPTER XVII. | - 67 - |
| THE REVENGEFUL NATURE OF THE HINDOO RELIGION. | - 67 - |

| | |
|---|---|
| CHAPTER XVIII. | - 69 - |
| THE DECEPTION OF THE HINDOOS. | - 69 - |
| CHAPTER XIX. | - 70 - |
| SUPERSTITION OF THE HINDOOS. | - 70 - |
| CHAPTER XX. | - 72 - |
| BURMAH, CHINA, ETC., ETC. | - 72 - |
| CHAPTER XXI. | - 77 - |
| THE DUTY OF PRAYING AND CONTRIBUTING FOR THE SPREAD OF THE GOSPEL. | - 77 - |
| CHAPTER XXII. | - 85 - |
| PERSONAL LABORS AMONG THE HEATHEN. | - 85 - |
| CHAPTER XXIII. | - 91 - |
| SUCCESS OF THE GOSPEL IN INDIA AND CEYLON. | - 91 - |

# CHAPTER I.

## GENERAL REMARKS

My dear children—When I was a little boy, my dear mother taught me, with the exception of the last line, the following prayer:

"Now I lay me down to sleep,I pray the Lord my soul to keep;If I should die before I wake,I pray the Lord my soul to take;And this I ask for Jesus' sake."

Though I am now more than fifty years old, I often like to say this prayer before I go to sleep. Have you ever learned it, my dear children? If you have not, I hope that you will learn it *now*; and I hope, too, that when you say your other prayers at night, you will also say this. I think that you would be glad to see how this prayer looks in the Tamul language—the language in which I am now preaching the Gospel, and in which I hope that some of you will hereafter tell the heathen of the Saviour. The following is a translation of it:

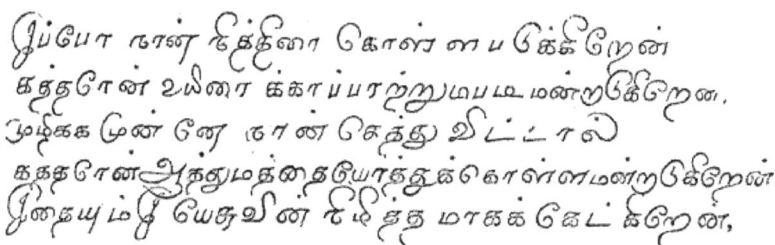

I wish that all the little heathen children knew this prayer; but their fathers and mothers do not teach it to them. Their fathers and mothers teach them to pray to gods of gold, or brass, or stone. They take them, while they are very young, to their temples, and teach them to put up their hands before an idol, and say, "Swammie." Swammie means Lord. As idolatry is the root of all sin, these children, as you may suppose, in early life become very wicked. They disobey their parents, speak bad words, call ill names, swear, steal, and tell lies. They also throw themselves on the ground in anger, and in their rage they tear their hair, or throw dirt over their heads, and do many other wicked things.

Let me give you an instance, to show you how they will speak bad words. A few months ago, a little girl about twelve years of age was brought to me, with two tumors in her back. To cut them out, I had to make an incision about eight inches in length; and as one of these tumors had extended under the shoulder-blade she suffered much before the operation was finished. While I was operating she cried out, "I will pull out my eyes." "I will pull out my tongue." "Kurn kertta tayvun." The translation of this is, "The blind-eyed god." By this expression, she meant to say, "What kind of a god are you, not to look upon me, and help me in my distress?" If this little girl had had a Christian father to teach her to love the Saviour, she would not have used such bad language. But this father was even more wicked than his daughter, inasmuch as those who grow old in sin, are worse than those who have not sinned so long. I never saw a more hard-hearted parent. That he was so, will appear from his conduct after the operation was finished. He left his daughter, and went off to his home, about forty miles distant. Before going, he said to his wife, or to one who came with her, "If the child gets well, bring her home; if she dies, take her away and bury her."

I hope, my dear children, that when you think of the wicked little girl just mentioned, you will be warned never to speak bad words. God will be very angry with you, if you do. Did you never read what is said in 2 Kings, 2d chapter and 23d verse, about the little children who mocked the prophet Elijah, and spoke bad words to him. O, how sorry must they have felt for their conduct, when they saw the paws of those great bears lifted up to tear them in pieces, and which did tear them in pieces. Besides all this, little children who speak bad words can never go to heaven. God will cast them into the great fire. Have you ever spoken bad words? If so, God is angry with you, and he will not forgive you unless you are sorry that you have done so, and seek his forgiveness through the blood of his dear Son.

# CHAPTER II.

## THE COLOR AND ORNAMENTS OF THE HINDOOS.

My dear children—If you will take a piece of mahogany in your hands, and view its different shades, you will have a pretty good representation of the color of a large class of this heathen people—I say, of a large class, for there is a great variety of colors. Some appear to be almost of a bronze color. Some are quite black. It is difficult to account for the different colors which we often see in the same family. For instance, one child will be of the reddish hue to which I just referred; another will be quite dark. When I was in Ceylon, two sisters of this description joined my church. One was called Sevappe, or the red one; the other was called Karappe, or the black one.

This people very much resemble the English and Americans in their features. Many of them are very beautiful. This remark will apply particularly to children, and more especially to the children of Brahmins and others, who are delicately brought up. But however beautiful any of this people may be, they try to make themselves appear more so, by the ornaments which they wear. These ornaments are of very different kinds, and are made of gold, silver, brass, precious stones, or glass. All are fond of ear-rings. Sometimes four or five are worn in each ear, consisting of solid gold, the lower one being the largest, and the upper one the smallest. Some men wear a gold ornament attached to the middle of the ear, in which a precious stone is inserted. Sometimes they wear very large circular ear-rings, made of the wire of copper, around which gold is twisted so as to cover every part of it. These are frequently ornamented with precious stones. The females, in addition to ear-rings, have an ornament which passes through the rim of the ear, near the head, half of it being seen above the rim, and half of it below it. An ornamental chain is sometimes attached to this, which goes some distance back, when it is lost in the hair. They sometimes also wear a jewel in the middle of the rim of the ear, and another on that little forward point which strikes your finger when you attempt to put it into the ear. Nose jewels also are worn. Sometimes three are worn at the same time. Holes are made through each side of the lower part of the nose, and through the cartilage, or that substance which divides the nostrils, through which they are suspended. The higher and wealthier females wear a profusion of ornaments of gold and pearls around the neck.

A very pretty ornament, about three inches in diameter, having the appearance of gold, is also frequently worn by them on that part of the head where the females in America put up their hair in a knot. In addition to this, the little girls sometimes wear one or two similar but smaller ornaments below this, as well as an ornament at the end of the long braid of hair which hangs down over the middle of their backs. Occasionally the whole, or the greater part of this braid is covered with an ornament of the same materials with those just described. They also wear an ornament extending from the crown of the head to the forehead, just in that spot where the little girls to whom I am writing part their hair. Attached to this, I have seen a circular piece of gold filled with rubies. Rings are worn on the toes as well as on the fingers, and bracelets of gold or silver on the wrists. Anklets similar to bracelets, and tinkling ornaments are worn on the ankles. The poor, who cannot afford to wear gold or silver bracelets, have them made of glass stained with different colors. I have seen nearly a dozen on each wrist.

The little boys wear gold or silver bracelets; also gold or silver anklets. I just alluded to finger-rings. I have seen a dozen on the same hand. In this part of the country, the little opening which is made in the ears of the children is gradually distended until it becomes very large. At first, the opening is only large enough to admit a wire. After this has been worn for a short time, a knife is introduced into the ear in the direction of the opening, and an incision made large enough to admit a little cotton. This is succeeded by a roll of oiled cloth, and by a peculiar shrub, the English name of which, if it has any, I do not know. When the hole becomes sufficiently large, a heavy ring of lead, about an inch in diameter, is introduced. This soon increases the size of the opening to such an extent, that a second, and afterwards a third, a fourth, and a fifth ring are added. By these weights, the lower parts of the ear are drawn down sometimes very nearly, or quite to the shoulders. Not unfrequently the little girls, when they run, are obliged to catch hold of these rings to prevent the injury which they would receive by their striking against their necks. I need hardly say, that in due time, these rings are removed, and ornamented rings are substituted.

A different plan is pursued with the Mohammedan little girls. They have their ears bored from the top to the bottom of the ear. The openings which are at first made are small, and are never enlarged. A ring is inserted in each of these openings. I have seen a little girl to-day in whose ears I counted twenty-four rings.

Flowers in great profusion are sometimes used to add to the adornment of the jewels.

I cannot conclude my account of the jewels of the little girls, without giving you a description of the appearance of a little patient of mine who came here a few days ago, loaded with trinkets. I will give it in the words of my daughter, which she wrote in part while the girl was here. "On the 17th, a little dancing-girl came to see us. She was adorned with many jewels, some of which were very beautiful. The jewel in the top of the ear was a circle, nearly the size of a dollar. It was set with rubies. Nine pearls were suspended from it. In the middle of the ear was a jewel of a diamond shape, set with rubies and pearls. The lowest jewel in the ear was shaped like a bell. It was set with rubies, and from it hung a row of pearls. Close by the ear, suspended from the hair, was a jewel which reached below her ear. It consisted of six bells of gold, one above the other. Around each was a small row of pearls, which reached nearly to the bell below, thus forming a jewel resembling very many drops of pearls. It is the most beautiful jewel that I ever saw. In the right side of her nose was a white stone, set with gold, in the shape of a star. From it hung a large pearl. There was a hole bored in the partition between the nostrils. This hole had a jewel in it, about an inch in length, in the middle of which was a white stone with a ruby on each side. It also had a ruby on the top. From the white stone hung another, of a similar color, attached to it by a piece of gold. In the left side of the nose was a jewel about an inch in diameter. It was somewhat in the shape of a half-moon, and was set with rubies, pearls, emeralds, etc. etc. This jewel hung below her mouth. On the back of her head was a large, round gold piece, three inches in diameter. Another piece about two inches in diameter, hung below this. Her hair was braided in one braid, and hung down her back. At the bottom of this were three large tassels of silk, mounted with gold. Her eyebrows and eyelashes were painted with black. Her neck was covered with jewels of such beauty, and of such a variety, that it is impossible for me to describe them. Around her ankles were large rings which looked like braided silver. To these were attached very many little bells, which rung as she walked. I believe all dancing-girls wear these rings. We felt very sad when we thought that she was dedicated to a life of infamy and shame."

There is an ornament worn by the followers of the god Siva, on their arms, or necks, or in their hair. It is called the *lingum*. The nature of this is so utterly abominable, that I cannot tell you a word about it.

Married women wear an ornament peculiar to themselves. It is called the tahly. It is a piece of gold, on which is engraven the image of some one of their gods. This is fastened around the neck by a short yellow string, containing one hundred and eight threads of great fineness. Various ceremonies are performed before it is applied, and the gods, of whom I will tell you something by and by, with their wives, are called upon to give their blessing. When these ceremonies are finished, the tahly is brought on a waiter, ornamented with sweet-smelling flowers, and is tied by the bridegroom to the neck of the bride. This ornament is never taken off, unless her husband dies. In such a case she is deprived of it, to wear it no more for ever—deprived of it, after various ceremonies, by her nearest female relative, who cuts the thread by which it is suspended, and removes it. After this a barber is called, who shaves her head, and she becomes, in the eyes of the people, a *despised* widow—no more to wear any ornament about her neck but a plain one—no more to stain her face with yellow water, nor to wear on her forehead those marks which are considered by the natives as among their chief ornaments.

I have now told you something about the jewels of this people. I hope that you will never be disposed to imitate them, and load your bodies with such useless things. They are not only useless, but tend to encourage pride and vanity. All that you need is, the "Pearl of great price," even Jesus. Adorn yourself with this Pearl, and you will be beautiful indeed—beautiful even in the sight of your heavenly Father. Have you this Pearl of great price, my dear children? Tell me, have you this Pearl of great price? If you have not, what have you?

I just now alluded to those marks which the natives consider among their chief ornaments. These are different among different sects. The followers of Siva rub ashes on their foreheads. These ashes are generally prepared by burning what in the Tamul language is called *chaarne*. They also apply these ashes in streaks, generally three together, on their breasts, and on their arms. Some besmear their whole bodies with them.

The followers of Vrishnoo wear a very different ornament from that just described. It consists of a perpendicular line drawn on the forehead, generally of a red or yellow color, and a white line on each side of it, which unite at the bottom with the middle line, and form a trident.

Another ornament consists of a small circle, which is called pottu. This is stamped in the middle of the forehead. Sometimes it is red, sometimes yellow or black. Large numbers of women, in this part of the country, wash their faces with a yellow water, made so by dissolving in it a paste made of a yellow root and common shell-lime. The Brahmins frequently instead of rubbing ashes, draw a horizontal line over the middle of their foreheads, to show that they have bathed and are pure. Sometimes the people ornament themselves with a paste of sandal-wood. They rub themselves from head to foot with it. This has a very odoriferous smell.

When the people are loaded with jewels, and covered with the marks which I have just described they think themselves to be highly ornamented But after all, "they are like unto whited sepulchres, which indeed appear beautiful outward, but are within full of dead men's bones, and of all uncleanness." The "Pearl of great price," to which I before alluded, the only Pearl which is of any value in the sight of Him who looketh at the heart, and not at the outward appearance, they possess not. Millions in this Eastern world have never even heard of it. O how incessantly ought you to pray that they may come into possession of it. How gladly should you give your money to send it to them. I wish, in this place, to ask you one question. Who of you expect, by and by, to become missionaries to this land, to tell this people of the Pearl of great price?

# CHAPTER III.

## DRESS, HOUSES, EATING, AND SALUTATION OF THE HINDOOS.

My dear Children—The dress of the Hindoos is very simple. A single piece of cloth uncut, about three yards in length and one in width, wrapped round the loins, with a shawl thrown over the shoulders, constitutes the usual apparel of the people of respectability. These garments are often fringed with red silk or gold. The native ladies frequently almost encase themselves in cloth or silk. Under such circumstances, their cloths are perhaps twenty yards in length. Most of the native gentlemen now wear turbans, an ornament which they have borrowed from the Mohammedans This consists of a long piece of very fine stuff, sometimes twenty yards in length and one in breadth. With this they encircle the head in many folds.

Those who are employed by European or Mohammedan princes, wear a long robe of muslin, or very fine cloth. This also, is in imitation of the Mohammedans, and was formerly unknown in the country.

The houses of the Hindoos are generally very plainly built. In the country, they are commonly made of earth, and thatched with straw. In the cities, they are covered with tiles. The kitchen is situated in the most retired part of the house. In the houses of the Brahmins, the kitchen-door is always barred, to prevent strangers from looking upon their earthen vessels; for if they should happen to see them, their look would pollute them to such a degree that they must be broken to pieces. The hearth is generally placed on the south-west side, which is said to be the side of the *god of fire*, because they say that this god actually dwells there.

The domestic customs of this people are very different from ours. The men and women do not eat together. The husband first eats, then the wife. The wife waits upon the husband After she has cooked the rice, she brings a brass plate, if they are possessors of one; or if not, a piece of a plantain-leaf, and puts it down on the mat before him. She then bails out the rice, places it upon the leaf, and afterwards pours the currie over it. This being done, the husband proceeds to mix up the currie and the rice with his hands, and puts it into his mouth. He never uses a knife and fork, as is customary with us. The currie of which I have spoken is a sauce of a yellow color, owing to the *munchel*, a yellow root which they put in it. This and onions, kottamaly-seeds mustard, serakum, pepper, etc., constitute the ingredients of the currie. Some add to these ghea, or melted butter, and cocoa-nut milk. By the cocoa-nut milk, I do not mean the water of the cocoa-nut. This—except in the very young cocoa-nut, when it is a most delicious beverage—is never used. The milk is squeezed from the *meat* of the cocoa-nut, after it has been reduced to a pulp by means of an indented circular iron which they use for this purpose.

After the husband has eaten, the wife brings water for him to wash his hands. This being done, she supplies him with vettalay, paakku, shell-lime, and tobacco, which he puts into his mouth as his dessert. The vettalay is a very spicy leaf. Why they use paakku, I do not know. It is a nut, which they cut into small pieces, but it has not much taste. Sometimes the wife brings her husband a segar. This people, I am sorry to say, are great smokers and chewers, practices of which I hope that you, my dear children, will never be guilty. In Ceylon, it is customary for females to smoke. Frequently, after the husband has smoked for a while, he hands the segar to his wife. She then puts it into her mouth, and smokes.

Several years ago, one of the schoolmasters in that island became a Christian. After he had partaken of the Lord's supper, his wife considered him so defiled, that she would not put his segar into her mouth for a month afterwards. She, however, has since become a Christian.

I spoke just now of the plantain-leaf. This leaf is sometimes six feet long, and in some places a foot and a half wide. It is an unbroken leaf, with a large stem running through the middle of it. It is one of the handsomest of leaves. Pieces enough can be torn from a single leaf, to take the place of a dozen plates. When quite young, it is an excellent application to surfaces which have been blistered.

When this people eat, they do not use tables and chairs. They sit down on mats, and double their legs under them, after the manner of our friends the tailors in America, when they sew. This is the way in which the natives as a general thing, sit in our churches. It is not common to have benches or pews for them. Carpenters and other tradesmen also sit down either on a board, or on the ground, or on their legs, when they work. It would divert you much to see their manoeuvring. If a carpenter, for instance, wants to make a little peg, he will take a small piece of board, and place it in an erect position between his feet, the soles of which are turned inward so as to press upon the board. He then takes his chisel in one hand, and his mallet in the other, and cuts off a small piece. Afterwards he holds the piece in one hand, and while he shapes it with his chisel with the other, he steadies it by pressing it against his great toe.

The blacksmiths, with the exception of those who use the sledge-hammer, sit as do the carpenters while they hammer the iron. I wish you could see them at work with their simple apparatus. They have small anvils, which they place in a hole made in a log of wood which is buried in the ground. They do not use such bellows as you see in America.

Theirs consist of two leather bags, about a foot wide and a foot and a half long, each having a nozzle at one end. The other end is left open to admit the air. When they wish to blow the fire, they extend these bags to let in the air. They then close them by means of the thumb on one side, and the fingers on the other, and press them down towards the nozzle of the bellows, which forces the air through them into the fire. I should have said before, that the nozzle of the bellows passes through a small semicircular mound of dried mud.

I mentioned that the natives do not use tables and chairs in their houses. Neither do they, as a general thing, use bedsteads. They have no beds. They sleep on mats, which are spread down on the floor. Sometimes they use a cotton bolster for their heads. More generally their pillows are hard boards, which they put under the mat. In addition to cooking, the females have to prepare the rice for this purpose, by taking it out of the husk. This they do by beating it in a mortar about two feet high. The pestle with which they pound it, is about five feet long, made of wood, with an iron rim around the lower part of it. Three women can work at these mortars at the same time. Of course they have to be very skilful in the use of the pestle, so as not to interfere with each others' operations. Sometimes, while thus engaged, the children, who are generally at play near their mothers, put their hands on the edge of the mortars. In such cases, when the pestle happens to strike the edge, their fingers are taken off in a moment.

The Hindoos have many modes of salutation. In some places they raise their right hand to the heart. In others, they simply stretch it out towards the person who is passing, if they know him, for they never salute persons with whom they are not acquainted.

In many places there is no show of salutation. When they meet their acquaintances they content themselves by saying a friendly word or two in passing, and then pursue their way. They have borrowed the word *salam* from the Mohammedans. They salute both Mohammedans and Europeans with this word, at the same time raising their hand to the forehead. When they address persons of high rank, they give them their *salam* thrice, touching the ground as often with both hands, and then lifting them up to their foreheads.

The other castes salute the Brahmins by joining the hands and elevating them to the forehead, or sometimes over the head. It is accompanied with *andamayya*, which means, Hail, respected lord. The Brahmins stretch out their hands and say, *aaseervaathum*—benediction.

Another very respectful kind of salutation consists in lowering both hands to the feet of the person to be honored, or even in falling-down and embracing them.

Of all the forms of salutation, the most respectful is the *shaashtaangkum*, or prostration, in which the feet, the knees, the stomach, the head, and the arms, all touch the ground. In doing this, they throw themselves at their whole length on the ground, and stretch out both arms above their heads. This is practised before priests, and in the presence of an assembly, when they appear before it to beg pardon for a crime.

Relations, who have long been separated, testify their joy when they meet by chucking each other under the chin, and shedding tears of joy. I am not aware that grown persons ever kiss each other. Sometimes mothers, or other individuals, will put their noses to the cheeks of little children, and draw the air through them, just as we do when we smell any thing which is agreeable. At other times they will apply the thumb and first finger to the cheek of the child, and then apply them to their own noses, and, as it were, smell them.

The women, as a mark of respect, turn their backs, or at least their faces aside, when they are in the presence of those whom they highly esteem. They are never permitted to sit in the presence of men. A married woman cannot do this, even in the presence of her husband.

If a person meets another of high rank, he must leave the path, if on foot, or alight, if on horseback, and remain standing until he has passed. He must at the same time take off his slippers. He also must take off his slippers when he enters a house. Should he fail to do this, it would be considered a great impropriety.

In addressing a person of note, they mast keep at a certain distance from him, and cover their mouths with their hands while they are speaking, lest their breath, or a particle of moisture, should escape to trouble him.

When the Hindoos visit a person of distinction for the first time, civility requires them to take some present as a mark of respect, or to show that they come with a friendly intention; especially if they wish to ask some favor in return. When they have not the means of making large presents, they carry with them sugar, plantains, milk, and other things of this kind.

In case of mourning, visits must always be made, though at a distance of a hundred miles. Letters of condolence would by no means be received as a substitute.

# CHAPTER IV.

## MARRIAGE AMONG THE HINDOOS.

My dear Children—Marriage, to the Hindoos is the greatest event of their lives. In the celebration of it, many ceremonies are performed Of these I will mention some of the most important. If the father of the young girl is a Brahmin, and if he is rich and liberal, he will frequently bear all the expenses of the marriage of his daughter. To give a daughter in marriage and to sell her, are about the same thing. Almost every parent makes his daughter an article of traffic, refusing to give her up until the sum of money for which he consented to let her go, is paid. Men of distinction generally lay out this money for jewels, which they present to their daughters on their wedding-day. You will infer from what I have just said, that the parties to be married have nothing to do in the choice of each other.

There are properly but four months in the year in which marriages can take place, namely March, April, May, and June. This probably arises from the circumstance that these are the hottest seasons of the year—the seasons when the people have more leisure to attend to them. From the harvest, also, which has just been gathered in, they are provided with means to perform the various ceremonies.

The marriage ceremony lasts five days. The bride and bridegroom are first placed under a puntel, a kind of bower, covered with leaves, in front of the house. This is superbly adorned. The married women then come forward, and perform the ceremony called *arati*, which is as follows. Upon a plate of copper, they place a lamp made of a paste from rice flour. It is supplied with oil, and lighted. They then take hold of the plate with both hands, and raise it as high as the heads of the couple to be married, and describe a number of circles with the plate and lamp. This is to prevent the evil of any jealous looks, which certain persons might make. The Hindoos believe that great evils arise from wicked looks. They consider that even the gods themselves are not out of the reach of malicious eyes; and therefore after they have been carried through the streets, the ceremony of arati is always performed, to efface the evil which they may have suffered from these looks.

It ought to have been mentioned, that before any thing is done, they place an image of Pullian under the puntel. This god is much honored because he is much feared. And although the great ugliness of his appearance has hitherto kept him without a wife, they never fail to pay him the greatest attention, lest he should in some way or other injure them.

After arati and many other ceremonies are performed, the kankanan, which is merely a bit of saffron, is tied to the right wrist of the young man, and to the left wrist of the girl. This is done with great solemnity. Another remarkable ceremony succeeds this. The young man being seated with his face towards the east, his future father-in-law supposes that he beholds in him the great Vrishnoo. With this impression, he offers him a sacrifice, and then, making him put both of his feet in a new dish filled with cow-dung, he first washes them with water, then with milk, and again with water, accompanying the whole with suitable muntrums or prayers.

After many other ceremonies, he takes the hand of his daughter and puts it into that of his son-in-law. He then pours water over them in honor of Vrishnoo. This is the most solemn of all the ceremonies, being the token of his resigning his daughter to the authority of the young man. She must be accompanied with three gifts, namely, one or more cows, some property in land, and a *salagrama*, which consists of some little amulet stones in high esteem among the Brahmins. This ceremony being finished, the tahly is brought to be fastened to the neck of the bride. This, as I before said, is presented on a salver, decked and garnished with sweet-smelling flowers. Incense is offered to it, and it is presented to the assistants each of whom touches it and invokes blessings upon it. The bride then turning towards the East, the bridegroom takes the tahly, repeats a muntrum or prayer aloud, and ties it around her neck.

Fire is then brought in, upon which the bridegroom offers up the sacrifice of *homam*, which consists of throwing boiled rice with melted butter upon the fire. He then takes his bride by the hand, and they walk three times around it, while the incense is blazing.

There is another ceremony, which, perhaps, ought to be mentioned, as it is considered by some to be one of much importance. Two baskets of bamboo are placed close together, one for the bride, the other for the bridegroom. They step into them, and two other baskets being brought, filled with ground rice, the husband takes up one with both hands and pours the contents over the head of the bride. She does the same to him. In the marriage of great princes pearls are sometimes used instead of rice.

On the evening of the third day, when the constellations appear, the astrologer points out to the married pair a very small star, close to the middle or in the tail of *Ursa Major*, which he directs them to worship, and which he says is the wife of Vasestha.

While the assembled guests, are dining, the bridegroom and the bride also partake, and eat together from the same plate. This is a token of the closest union. This is the only instance in which they ever eat together.

After all the ceremonies are finished, a procession is made through the streets of the village It commonly takes place in the night, by torchlight, accompanied with fire-works. The newly married pair are seated in one palanquin with their faces towards each other, both richly dressed. The bride, in particular, is generally covered with jewels and precious stones.

The procession moves slowly; and their friends and relations come out of their houses, as they pass; the women hailing the married couple with the ceremony of *arati*, and the men with presents of silver, fruits, sugar, and betel. I once witnessed one of these marriage processions in the streets of Madras at night, but can give you but little idea of its magnificence. The lamps used on the occasion could not be numbered. The shrubbery, which was drawn on carts or other vehicles, appeared exceedingly beautiful, in consequence of the light reflected from the lamps. Intermingled with this shrubbery, were to be seen little girls elegantly dressed, and adorned with flowers on their heads. Many elephants, with their trappings of gold and silver and red, formed a part of the procession. Fire-works were also added to make the scene more brilliant.

# CHAPTER V.

## DEATH AND FUNERALS OF THE HINDOOS.

My dear Children—The death of a Hindoo is followed by many ridiculous ceremonies. I will give you a description of a few, connected with the death of one who has moved in one of the higher ranks—of a Brahmin.

When it is evident that a Brahmin has but a little time to live, a space is prepared with earth, well spread with cow-dung, over which a cloth, that has never been worn, is spread. The dying man is placed upon this at full length. Another cloth is wrapped around his loins. This being done, the ceremony of expiating his sins is performed as follows. The chief of the funeral brings on one plate some small pieces of silver or copper coin, and on another the punchakaryam, etc. A little of this punchakaryam is then put into his mouth, and, by virtue of this nauseous draught, the body is perfectly purified. Besides this, there is a general cleansing, which is accomplished by making the dying man recite within himself, if he cannot speak, the proper muntrums, by which he is delivered from all his sins. After this, a cow is introduced with her calf. Her horns are decorated with rings of gold or brass, and her neck with garlands of flowers. A pure cloth is laid over her body. Thus decked, she is led up to the sick man, who takes hold of her tail. Prayers are now offered up that the cow may conduct him, by a blessed path, to the next world. He then makes a gift of a cow to a Brahmin. This gift is considered indispensable to enable the soul to go over the river of fire, which it is said all must pass after death. Those who have made this gift, are met by one of these favored creatures the moment they arrive at the bank of the stream, and by her help, they are enabled to pass without injury from the flames.

As soon as the breath has left his body, all who are present must weep for a reasonable time, and join in lamentations together.

After various ceremonies, the body is washed, and a barber is called to shave his head. He is then clad with his finest clothes and adorned with jewels. He is rubbed with sandal-wood where the body is uncovered, and the accustomed mark is put upon his forehead. Thus dressed he is placed on a kind of state bed, where he remains until he is carried to the pile.

After every preparation is made to bear away the corpse, the person who is to conduct the funeral, with the assistance of some relative or friend, strips it of its clothing and jewels, and covers it with a handkerchief provided for the occasion. The corpse is then placed on a litter. Those who die in a state of marriage, have their faces left uncovered. The litter, adorned with flowers and foliage, and sometimes decked with valuable stuffs, is borne by four Brahmins. The procession is arranged as follows.

The chief of the funeral marches foremost, carrying fire in a vessel. The body follows, attended by the relations and friends, without their turbans, and with nothing on their heads but a bit of cloth, in token of mourning. The women never attend the funeral, but remain in the house, where they set up a hideous cry when the corpse is taken out. While advancing on the road, the custom is to stop three times on the way, and, at each pause, to put into the mouth of the dead a morsel of unboiled rice, moistened. The object of stopping is considered to be very important. It is not without reason; for they say that persons supposed to be dead have been alive, or even when lifeless have been restored; and sometimes, also, it has happened that the gods of the infernal regions have mistaken their aim, and seized one person instead of another. In any view, it is right to afford the opportunity for correcting these mistakes, so as not to expose to the flames a person who is still alive. Hence the propriety of these pauses, each of which continues half of the quarter of an hour.

Having arrived at the place for burning the dead, they dig a trench about six or seven feet in length. This is consecrated by the muntrums. It is slightly sprinkled with water to lay the dust, and a few pieces of money in gold are scattered upon it. Here the pile is erected of dried wood, on which the body is laid out at full length. Over the body a quantity of twigs are laid, which are sprinkled with punchakaryam The chief of the funeral then takes on his shoulders a pitcher of water, and goes around the pile three times, letting the water run through a hole made in it. After this he breaks the pitcher in pieces near the head of the corpse.

At last the torch is brought for setting fire to the pile, and is handed to the chief of the funeral. Before he receives it, however, he is obliged to make some grimaces to prove his sorrow. He rolls about on the ground, beats his breast, and makes the air resound with his cries. The assistants also cry, or appear to cry. Fire being applied to the four corners of the pile, the crowd retire, except the four Brahmins who carried the body; they remain until the whole is consumed.

The funerals of the Sudras differ in some particulars from those of the Brahmins. Deafening sounds of drums, trumpets, and other instruments of music, not in use among the Brahmins, accompany their funerals. To increase the noise, they sometimes shoot off an instrument which somewhat resembles a small cannon. I do not now think of any other particular worthy of mention.

By the ceremonies which are performed at their funerals, this wretched people expect to secure the pardon of all the sins of those who have died. Alas, what a delusion! O, that Christians had sent the Gospel to this dark land in the days when they sent it to our heathen fathers. Then might the Hindoos now be seeking the expiation of their sins, through the blood of the ever-blessed Redeemer. Of this Redeemer, however, they know nothing. They enter eternity, not that their souls may be consumed as their bodies have been, but to endure the flames of divine wrath for ever and ever. Alas, alas, that it should be so! O, that the generation of Christians now living would lay these things to heart, and do what they can, through grace, to rescue those who are yet within the reach of hope from so tremendous a doom. What, my dear children, will you do for this purpose?

# CHAPTER VI.

## THE GODS OF THE HINDOOS.

My dear Children—The word heathen is applied to those who worship idols, or who do not know any thing about the true God. This is the case with this people. They say that there is one supreme being, whom they call BRAHM; but he is very different from Jehovah, and is never worshipped. Generally, he is fast asleep. In the place of Brahm, they worship many gods—gods of all colors: some black, some white, some blue, some red—gods of all shapes and sizes: some in the shape of beasts, some in the shape of men; some partly in the shape of beasts, and partly in the shape of men, having four, or ten, or a hundred, or a thousand eyes, heads, and hands. They ride through the air on elephants, buffaloes, lions, sheep, deer, goats, peacocks, vultures, geese, serpents, and rats. They hold in their hands all kinds of weapons, offensive and defensive, thunderbolts javelins, spears, clubs, bows, arrows, shields, flags, and shells. They are of all employments. There are gods of the heavens above and of the earth below, gods of wisdom and of folly, gods of war and of peace, gods of good and of evil, gods of pleasure, gods of cruelty and wrath, whose thirst must be satiated with torrents of blood. These gods fight and quarrel with one another. They lie, steal, commit adultery, murder, and other crimes. They pour out their curses when they cannot succeed in their wicked plots, and invent all kinds of lying tales to hide their wickedness.

There are three principal gods, who compose what is called the Hindoo triad. Their names are Brumha, Vrishnoo, and Siva. They were somehow drawn from Brahm's essence, on one occasion when he was awake. Brumha, they say, is the creator of the world, Vrishnoo the preserver, and Siva the destroyer. Brumha has no temple erected for his worship, on account of a great falsehood which he told. I will tell you what it was. Once, as it is said, there was a dispute between him and Vrishnoo, as to who is the greatest. While thus disputing, Siva appeared between the two as a fire-post and told them that he who would find the bottom or the top of the post first, would show that he is the greatest. Vrishnoo immediately changed himself into a hog, and began to root up the earth with the hope of finding the bottom of the post. Brumha changed himself into a swan, flew up towards the top of the post, and cried out, I have found it, when he had not. This, you know, my dear children, was a falsehood. For this falsehood, it is said, no temple is erected for his worship.

Vrishnoo was a thief and a liar. He was once dwelling in the house of a dairyman, and he used constantly to be stealing butter and curdled milk from the dairyman's wife. She did not know, for a long time, what became of her butter and curdled milk; but at last she found out that Vrishnoo was the thief. To punish him for his theft, she tied him to a rice mortar.

Siva's conduct was very bad. I will tell you but one thing about him. On one occasion he was playing at cards with his wife Parvathe. Vrishnoo was appointed to determine who was the best player. After playing for a little season Parvathe won the game. Siva then beckoned to Vrishnoo to declare that he, instead of Parvathe, had won it. This he did. In consequence of this falsehood, he was cursed by Parvathe, and changed into a snake.

And now, my dear children, why do I tell you about these gods? I tell you for the purpose of making you thankful that you were born in a Christian land, where you have the Bible to teach you better things. Had you not the Bible, you would worship just such wretched beings as these poor Hindoos worship. Perhaps you know that our Saxon fathers, before they had the Bible, were as great idolaters as are this people. They worshipped Thor and Woden and other similar idols, and they were even in the habit of offering up human sacrifices Surely, if there is any thing which should make you give your hearts to your Saviour and love him above all things, it is God's gift of the Bible to you.

# CHAPTER VII.

## THE THREE HUNDRED AND THIRTY MILLIONS OF THE GODS OF THE HINDOOS—THE CREATION OF THE UNIVERSE—THE TRANSMIGRATION OF SOULS—THE DIFFERENT HELLS.

My dear children—I told you that in one of those seasons when Brahm was awake, Brumha, Vrishnoo, and Siva were somehow drawn from Brahm's essence. The three hundred and thirty millions of the gods of the Hindoos were also drawn from this essence; as were all the atoms which compose the earth, the sun, moon, and stars. At first, these atoms were all in disorder. For the purpose of reducing them to order, Brahm created what is called the great mundane egg. Into this egg he himself entered, under the form, of Brumha, taking with him all these atoms. After remaining in this egg four thousand three hundred millions of years, to arrange these atoms, he burst its shell and came out, with a thousand heads, a thousand eyes, and a thousand arms. With him, he brought out all those harmonized atoms, which, when separated, produced this beautiful universe that we see above and around us.

The universe, as it came from the mundane egg, is generally divided into fourteen worlds: seven inferior or lower worlds, and seven superior or upper worlds. The seven lower worlds are filled with all kinds of wicked and loathsome creatures. Our earth, which is the first of the upper worlds, it is said, is flat. The following figure will give you some idea of it.

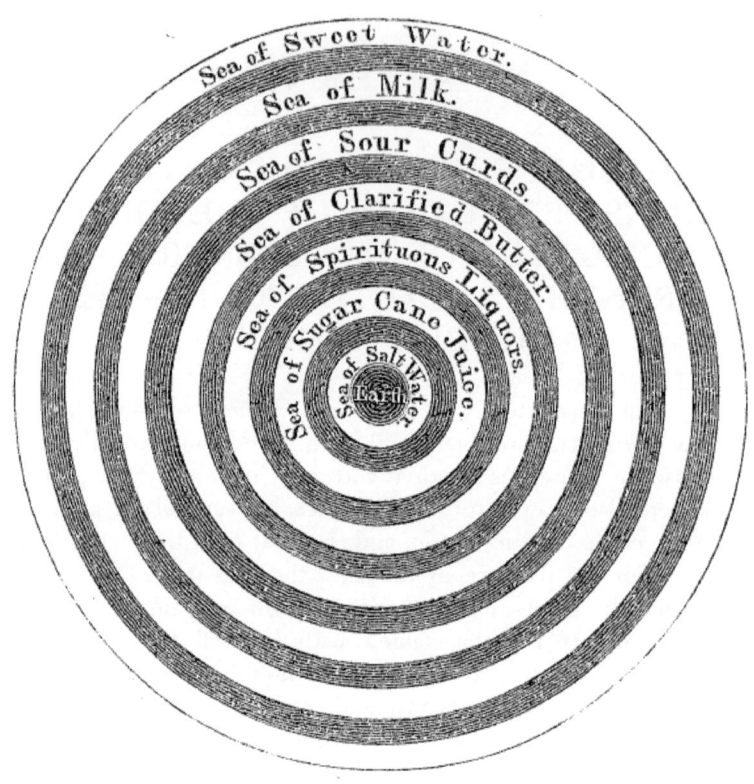

That part of the earth which is inhabited consists of seven circular islands, or continents each of which is surrounded by a different ocean. The island in the centre, where we dwell, is surrounded by a sea of salt water, the second island is surrounded by a sea of sugar-cane juice, the third island is surrounded by a sea of spirituous liquors, the fourth is surrounded by a sea of clarified butter, the fifth is surrounded by a sea of sour curds, the sixth is surrounded by a sea of milk, the seventh is surrounded by a sea of sweet water.

In all the worlds above ours are mansions where the gods reside. In the third is the heaven of Indra. This is the heaven to which it is said the widow goes, after she has burned herself to death on the funeral pile of her husband Its palaces are of the purest gold. And such are the quantities of diamonds, and jasper, and sapphire, and emerald, and all manner of precious stones there, that it shines with a brightness superior to that of twelve thousand suns. Its streets are of the clearest crystal, fringed with gold. In the seventh, or the highest of the upper worlds, is the heaven where Brumha chiefly resides. This far exceeds all the other heavens in point of beauty.

In the inferior worlds it is stated that there are one hundred thousand hells. These are provided for such as have been great criminals. The Hindoos say, that those who have not been very wicked, can make an atonement for their sins in this world. Should they neglect to do this, they must suffer for it in another birth. They believe in what is called the transmigration of souls, or the passing of the soul, after death, into another body. The soul must suffer in the next birth, if not purified in this. Hence it is asserted, that if a man is a stealer of gold from a Brahmin, he is doomed to have whitlows on his nails; if a drinker of spirits, black teeth; if a false detractor, fetid breath; if a stealer of grain, the defect of some limb; if a stealer of clothes, leprosy; if a horse-stealer, lameness; if a stealer of a lamp, total blindness. If he steals grain in the husk, he will be born a rat; if yellow mixed metal, a gander; if money, a great stinging gnat; if fruit, an ape; if the property of a priest, a crocodile.

Those persons whose sins are too great to be forgiven in this world, must be sent to one of the hells to winch I have alluded. Weeping, wailing, shrieking, they are dragged to the palace of *Yama*, the king of those doleful regions. On arriving there, they behold him clothed with terror, two hundred and forty miles in height, his eyes as large as a lake of water, his voice as loud as thunder, the hairs of his body as long as palm-trees, a flame of fire proceeding from his mouth, the noise of his breath like the roaring of a tempest, and in his right hand a terrific iron club. Sentence is passed, and the wretched beings are doomed to receive punishment according to the nature of their crimes. Some are made to tread on burning sands, or sharp-edged stones. Others are rolled among thorns and spikes and putrefying flesh. Others are dragged along the roughest places by cords passed through the tender parts of the body. Some are attacked by jackals, tigers, and elephants. Others are pierced with arrows, beaten with clubs, pricked with needles, seared with hot irons, and tormented by flies and wasps. Some are plunged into pans of liquid fire or boiling oil. Others are dashed from lofty trees, many hundred miles high.

The torment of these hells does not continue for ever. After criminals have been punished for a longer or shorter time, their souls return to the earth again in the bodies of men. Here they may perform such good acts as may raise them to one of the heavens of the gods; or commit crimes, which may be the means of their being sent again to the abodes of misery.

Things will go on in this way until the universe comes to an end, when every thing is to disappear, and to be swallowed up in Brahm.

The Hindoos say, that it is now more than one hundred and fifty billions of years since the world was created. After it has continued about one hundred and fifty billions of years more, it is to come to an end. Then Brumha is to die, and to be swallowed up with the universe in the sole existing Brahm.

By what you have heard, you will learn that the Hindoos expect, by their sufferings, to make an atonement for their sins. But there is no atonement for sin, except through the blood of Jesus Christ. We must come as lost sinners to our heavenly Father, confess our transgressions to him, and plead for his forgiveness, only through the sufferings and death which Christ endured. My dear children, have you done this? If not, do it speedily, or the regions of the lost must soon be your everlasting abode.

# CHAPTER VIII.

## HINDOO CASTES.

My dear Children—The people of India are divided into castes, as they are called. Their sacred books declare, that after Brumha had peopled the heavens above and the worlds below, he created the human race, consisting of four classes or castes. From his mouth proceeded the Brahmin caste. Those of this class are the highest and noblest beings on earth, and hold the office of priests. At the same time there flowed from his mouth the *Vedas*, or sacred books, of which the Brahmins are the sole teachers To their fellow-men, they were to give such parts of these books as they thought best. From Brumha's arm proceeded the military caste. The business of this class is to defend their country when attacked by enemies. From his breast proceeded the third caste, consisting of farmers and merchants. From his feet, the member of inferiority, proceeded the Sudras, or servile caste. Carpenters, braziers, weavers, dyers, and the manual cultivators of the soil, are included in this class.

Caste is not a civil, but a sacred institution. You must get some one older than yourself to explain what this means. Caste is a difference of *kind*. Hence, a man of one caste can never be changed into a man of another caste, any more than a lion can be changed into a mole, or a mole into a lion. Each caste has its laws, the breaking of which is attended with great disgrace, and even degradation below all the other castes. For instance, if a Brahmin should, by eating any forbidden thing, break his caste, he would sink below all the other castes. He would become an outcast, or pariah. For beneath the fourth, or lowest caste, there is a class of people belonging to no caste—a class of outcasts, held in the utmost abhorrence.

By the system of castes, the Hindoos have been divided into so many selfish sections, each scowling on all the rest with feelings of hatred and contempt. The spirit which upholds it, is similar to that spirit which says, "Stand by thyself, for I am holier than thou," and, of course, is nothing but pride. This is one of the greatest obstacles to the spread of Christianity in this dark land, and for the exhibition of which we were lately obliged to cut off many of the members of our churches.

The Brahmins, in consequence of their being of the highest caste, and of their having been taught from their infancy to regard all other classes of men with the utmost contempt, are very proud. They make great efforts to keep themselves pure, in their sense of the word, both without and within.

They are exceedingly afraid of being defiled by persons of other castes. They have the utmost dread even of being touched by a pariah. For them to eat with any of these pariahs, or to go into their houses, or to drink water which they have drawn, or from vessels which they have handled, is attended with the loss of their caste. A Brahmin who should enter their houses, or permit them to enter his, would be cut off from his caste, and could not be restored without many troublesome ceremonies and great expense. The pariahs are considered to be so low, that if a Brahmin were to touch them, even with the end of a long pole, he would be looked upon as polluted In some districts they are obliged to make a long circuit, when they perceive Brahmins in the way, that their breath may not infect them, or their shadow fall upon them as they pass. In some places their very approach is sufficient to pollute a whole neighborhood.

The Brahmins carry their ideas of purity very far. Should a Sudra happen to look upon the vessels in which they cook their food, they would be considered as defiled. They can never touch any kind of leather or skin, except the skin of the tiger and antelope. The most disagreeable of all American fashions, in their eyes, is that of boots and gloves. They rarely eat their food from plates; and when they do so, it is only at home. They use the leaf of the plantain or other trees as a substitute. To offer them any thing to eat on a metal or earthen plate which others have used, would be considered a great affront. For the same reason, they will neither use a spoon nor a fork when they eat; and they are astonished that any one, after having applied them to their mouths, and infected them with saliva, should repeat the act a second time. They have a great abhorrence of the toothpick, if used a second time. When they eat any thing dry, they throw it into their mouths, so that the fingers may not approach the lips.

They do not drink as we do, by applying the cup to the lips. This would be considered a gross impropriety. They pour the water into their months. The reason why they do these things is, because they consider the saliva to be the most filthy secretion that comes from the body. It is on this account that no one is ever permitted to spit within doors.

The use of animal food they consider to be defiling. Not only will they not eat animal food, but they will eat nothing that has the principle of life in it. On this account, they cannot eat eggs of any kind. I was once breaking an egg in my medicine-room at Panditeripo, while a Brahmin was present. He told me that, under such circumstances, he could not remain with me any longer. In his view, I was committing a great sin. To kill an ox or a cow, is considered by them as a crime which can never be atoned for, and to eat their flesh is a defilement which can never be washed away. To kill a cow is, by *Hindoo* law, punishable with death.

The touch of most animals, particularly that of the dog, defiles a Brahmin. Should a dog touch them, they would be obliged instantly to plunge into water, and wash their clothes, in order to get rid of such a stain. Notwithstanding this, the dog is one of the gods worshipped by the Hindoos.

The Hindoos consider themselves to be unclean if they have assisted at a funeral. When the ceremony is over, they immediately plunge into water for the sake of purification. Even the news of the death of a relative, a hundred miles off, has the same effect. The person who hears such news is considered unclean until he has bathed. In unison with this feeling, a person is no sooner dead, than he is hastened away to be buried or burned; for, until this is done, those in the house can neither eat nor drink, nor go on with their occupations.

A Brahmin who is particular in his delicacy, must be careful what he treads upon. He is obliged to wash his body or bathe, if he happens to tread on a bone, or a broken pot, a bit of rag, or a leaf from which one has been eating. He must also be careful where he sits down. Some devotees always carry their seats with them, that is, a tiger or antelope's skin, which are always held pure. Some are contented with a mat. They may sit down on the ground without defilement, provided it has been newly rubbed over with cow-dung. This last specific is used daily to purify their houses from the defilement occasioned by comers, and goers. When thus applied, diluted with water, it has unquestionably one good effect. It completely destroys the fleas and other insects, with which they are very much annoyed.

There is one thing more which I wish to mention. It is, that all the high castes consider the use of intoxicating drinks to be defiling. I hope that you, my dear children, will always have the same opinion, and never touch them any sooner than you would touch arsenic or other poisons.

A person may be restored to his caste, provided he has not committed an unpardonable offence. This is done as follows. After he has gained the consent of his relations to be restored he prostrates himself very humbly before them, they being assembled for that purpose, and submits to the blows or other punishment which they may think proper to inflict, or pays the fine which they may have laid upon him. Then, after shedding tears of sorrow, and making promises that, by his future conduct, he will wipe away the stain of his expulsion from caste, he makes the shaashtaangkum before the assembly. This being done, he is declared fit to be restored to his tribe.

When a man has been expelled from his caste for some great offence, those who restore him sometimes slightly burn his tongue with a piece of gold made hot. They likewise apply to different parts of the body redhot iron stamps, which leave marks that remain for ever. Sometimes they compel the offender to walk on burning embers; and to complete the purification, he must drink the punchakaryam, which literally means the *five things*; these all come from the cow, and must be mixed together. The first three of these I will mention, namely, the milk, butter, and curds. The other two, for the sake of delicacy, I must not mention. After the ceremony of punchakaryam is finished the person who has been expelled from his caste must give a grand feast. This finishes all he has to do, and he is then restored to favor.

There are certain offences which, when committed cut off all hope that the offender will ever be restored to his caste. For instance, should he eat the flesh of the cow, no presents which he might make, nor any fines which he might be disposed to pay, no, not even the punchakaryam itself, would be of any avail for his restoration or purification.

I will make a remark here, which I might have made before. It is, that in Christian countries, there is a spirit of pride which much resembles the spirit of caste. Many are to be found who are very proud that they have descended from rich and honorable *ancestors*, and who look down, almost with disdain, upon those in other situations. I need hardly tell you that this is a very wicked spirit, and entirely opposed to the spirit of the Gospel. No matter what may be our high thoughts of ourselves, we appear but very low in the sight of Him who created us. We are all sinners, and, as such, are offensive in his sight. If we would go to heaven, the first thing which we have to do, is to humble ourselves for the pride of our hearts, and become as little children before him. We must have that spirit of which the apostle speaks, when he says, "Let each esteem others better than themselves." With a humble spirit we may approach a holy God, with the assurance that he will, for Christ's sake, forgive all our sins.

# CHAPTER IX.

## HINDOO TEMPLES—CARS—PROCESSION OF IDOLS.

My dear Children—I will proceed to give you a description of the Hindoo temples. These are very numerous. One is to be found in almost every village. They are to be found, also, in out-of-the-way places, distant from villages, in woods, on the banks and in the middle of rivers; but, above all, on mountains and steep rocks.

This latter practice, of building temples on mountains, is very ancient. The Israelites were accustomed to choose a mountain when they offered up their sacrifices to the Lord. Solomon, before the building of the temple, chose Mount Gibeon on which to offer his burnt-offerings; and when the ten tribes separated themselves, in the reign of Jeroboam, they built their altars on the mountain of Samaria. This practice may have come from the circumstance, that Noah offered to God a great sacrifice of thanks on one of the highest mountains of Armenia. Probably Mount Ararat continued long to be remembered, by him and his descendants, as the scene of their deliverance.

Besides the temples of the idols, there are various objects of worship, made of earth and stone. Some of the idols are carved. Some consist merely of the rough stone. These are to be seen on the high-roads, at the entrance into villages, and, above all, under lofty trees. Some of these are covered; but generally they are exposed in the open air.

You will read in Genesis, 28th chap, and 18th verse, that Jacob, after his dream, rose up early in the morning and took the stone that he had put for his pillow, and set it up for a pillar, and poured oil upon the top of it. Whether it has happened from this circumstance or not, that the heathen universally pour oil over their idols, I cannot tell. All I know is, that they do it. No idol can become an object of worship until a Brahmin has said his muntrums, or prayers, for the purpose of bringing down the god to live, as it is said be does, in the image, and until he has drenched it with oil and liquid butter.

The idols, in the great temples, are clothed with rich garments, and adorned with jewels, which are enriched with precious stones of immense value. Sacrifices are constantly made to these idols, consisting of boiled rice, flowers, fruits, etc., but, above all, of lamps, of which many thousands are sometimes seen burning. They feed them with butter, in preference to oil.

The priests of the temples offer up sacrifices twice every day, morning and evening. They begin the ceremony by washing their idol. The water which is used is brought from a river or tank. Every morning a procession, with music, passes before our door, with this water.

Every priest who offers up sacrifices, must have several lighted lamps with a bell, which he holds in his left hand. With his right hand he makes an offering to the idol, adorns it with flowers, and rubs its forehead and various parts of its body with sandal-wood and holy ashes. While all this is going on, he is alone in the temple, the door of which is closed. The unholy multitude remain without, silently waiting till he has done. What he does, they cannot know, only hearing the sound of the bell. When he has done, he comes out and distributes among the people a part of the things which have been offered to the idol. These are considered as holy. If they consist of rice and fruit, they are immediately eaten; if of flowers, the men put them in their turbans, and the girls entwine them in their hair.

Next to the priests, the most important persons about the temples are the dancing girls. These are persons of the vilest character. They perform their religious duties in the temple twice a day. They also assist at the public ceremonies, and dance. At the same time they sing the most abominable and filthy songs. Of these wicked creatures, however, I must not tell you any thing further.

The next order of persons employed in the temples, are players on musical instruments. Every temple of note has a band of these musicians who, as well as the dancers, are obliged to attend the temple twice a day. They are also obliged to assist at all the public festivals. Their band generally consists of wind, instruments, resembling clarionets and hautboys, to which they add cymbals and drums. They have a bass, produced by blowing into a kind of tube, widened below, and which gives an uninterrupted sound. Part of the musicians sing hymns in honor of their gods.

The expenses of the temples are borne by the voluntary offerings of the people, consisting of money, jewels, cattle, provisions, and other articles. In order to induce them to make such offerings, the Brahmins use all kinds of deception. Sometimes they will put their idols in irons, chaining their hands and feet. They exhibit them in this sad condition, declaring that they have been brought into it by creditors from whom their gods had to borrow money, in times of trouble, to supply their wants. They declare that their creditors refuse to set the gods at liberty, until the money with the interest is paid. The people, seeing the deplorable condition into which they have been brought, come forward and pay off the debt; when the chains are taken off, and the god is set at liberty.

Another way in which the Brahmins sometimes deceive the people, is as follows. They say that the god is afflicted with some dreadful disease, brought on by the distress which he has had, because the people do not worship him as much as they should. In such cases, the idol is sometimes placed at the door of the temple where they rub his forehead and temples with various kinds of medicine. They also set before him all sorts of medicines, pretending in this way to do all they can to cure him. But as all their efforts prove to be vain, and the disease becomes worse, the Brahmins send out persons to tell the sad news. The people, believing the report, hasten to bring in their gifts and offerings. The god, on beholding such proofs of their attachment to him, feels himself cured of his disease, and immediately returns to his throne within the temple.

The Brahmins use another kind of deception, in order to procure offerings for the temples. They declare that their gods are angry with certain individuals who have offended them, and that they have sent some evil spirit or devil to take possession of their bodies and torment them. Accordingly, persons appear wandering about in different parts of the country, showing, by their dreadful convulsions, their writhings and twistings, every symptom of being possessed with the devil. The people who see them are filled with dismay, fall down before them, and offer gifts and sacrifices, for fear of being injured by them. Whatever they ask is granted. The people give them to eat and drink abundantly; and when they leave a place, accompany them with instruments of music, till they arrive at some other place, where the same deception is practised.

There are various other ways in which the Brahmins deceive the people; but I have told you enough.

At every large temple, there is at least yearly one grand procession. The idol is brought out from its inclosure, and placed in a great car or chariot, prepared for this express purpose. This stands upon four wheels of great strength, not made like ours, of spokes with a rim, but of three or four pieces of thick, solid timber, rounded and fitted to each other. The car is sometimes forty or fifty feet high, having upon it carved images of a most abominable nature. I must not tell you any thing about them. The car, when finished, presents somewhat the shape of a pyramid.

On the day of the procession, it is adorned with painted cloth, garlands of flowers, green shrubbery, and precious stuffs. The idol is placed in the centre, loaded with jewels, etc., to attract the attention of the people. Having fastened ropes to this enormous car, eight or nine hundred or a thousand people catch hold of the ropes and slowly drag it along, accompanied with the awful roaring of their voices. At certain periods they stop; when the immense crowds, collected from all parts of the country, set up one universal shout, or rather yell. This, with the sound of their instruments and numerous drums, produces much uproar and confusion. Sometimes the weighty car comes to a stand, from the dampness of the ground or from the narrowness of the streets, when the tumult and noise are redoubled.

Perhaps you know that on some occasions, when the cars are drawn, people throw themselves under the wheels, and are crushed to death. This occurs at the drawing of the car of Juggernaut, as you may learn if you will read my Sermon to Children, on the Condition of the Heathen. Here is a picture of Juggernaut, and on the last page you may see a picture of his car, and two men crushed to death under the wheels. Not long since, five persons were thus crushed to death. Many dreadful accidents also take place at the drawing of these cars. A few years ago several persons in this city had their limbs amputated, in consequence of injuries received.

When I was in America, I showed to many of the dear children an idol called Pulliar, which was *formerly* worshipped by Raamu, one of our native helpers, when he was a heathen. I gave a particular description, of the I manner in which he daily worshiped it, in the sermon above mentioned Here is a picture, which will give you some idea of this god.

You will see that it is partly in the shape of a man, and partly in the shape of a beast. You, my dear children, would put no confidence in such vain idols; but this people do, as you may know from what I am now going to tell you.

Some months ago, a woman was brought to me with a cancer in her breast. It had made sad ravages. On the morning after her arrival I took it out. Before she was brought to me, her brother went to the temple of the goddess Meenaache, to ascertain what was her will respecting his bringing her to me, or taking her to a native doctor. In order to ascertain it, he had recourse to the following expedient. He prepared several bundles of red and white flowers—the red to represent the red or Tamil man, the white to represent the white man. These flowers were carefully inclosed in leaves, so as to prevent their color being seen, and then laid down on the ground, at the entrance of the temple. After this, he called a little child to him, and then proceeded to entreat Meenaache that, if it were her will that he should bring the sick woman to me, she would direct the child to take up one of the parcels containing the white flowers. It so happened that the child took up one of these parcels. Of course, he brought her to me. Had it taken up a parcel containing the red flowers, she would have been taken to a native doctor. May we not hope that, not Meenaache, but Jehovah directed him to bring her to me, that she might hear of a very different being from her goddess, even of Jesus. Of him she has fully heard.

# CHAPTER X.

## FESTIVALS OF THE HINDOOS.

My dear Children—The Hindoos have many festivals. These are all occasions of joy and gladness. On such days, the people quit their usual employments. Friends and relations unite in family parties, and give entertainments according to their means. Innocent pastimes and amusements of various kinds are resorted too to add to their happiness.

There are eighteen principal festivals yearly, and no month passes without one or more of them.

One of the most solemn of these ceremonies is held in the month of September, and appears to be principally in honor of Parvathe, the wife of Siva. At this time every laborer and every artisan offers sacrifices and prayers to his tools. The laborer brings his plough, hoe, and other farming utensils. He piles them together, and offers a sacrifice to them, consisting of flowers, fruit, rice, and other articles. After this, he prostrates himself before them at full length, and then returns them to their places.

The mason offers the same adoration and sacrifice to his trowel, rule, and other instruments The carpenter adores his hatchet, adze, and plane. The barber collects his razors together and worships them with similar rites.

The writing-master sacrifices to the iron pen or style, with which he writes upon the palm-leaf the tailor to his needles, the weaver to his loom, the butcher to his cleaver.

The women, on this day, collect into a heap their baskets, rice-mill, rice-pounder, and other household utensils, and, after having offered sacrifices to them, fall down in adoration before them. Every person, in short, in this solemnity sanctifies and adores the instrument or tool by which he gains a living. The tools are considered as so many gods, to whom they present their prayers that they will continue to furnish them still with the means of getting a livelihood.

This least is concluded by making an idol to represent Parvathe. It is made of the paste of grain, and being placed under a sort of canopy, is carried through the streets with great pomp, and receives the worship of the people.

Another festival of great celebrity is observed in October. At this time, each person, for himself, makes offerings of boiled rice and other food, to such of their relations as have died, that they may have a good meal on that day. They afterwards offer sacrifices of burning lamps, of fruit, and of flowers, and also new articles of dress, that their ancestors may be freshly clothed.

At this festival, soldiers offer sacrifices to their weapons, in order to obtain success in war. On such occasions, a ram is offered in sacrifice to their armor.

In November, a festival is observed, which is called the feast of lamps. At this season, the Hindoos light lamps, and place them around the doors of their houses. This festival was established to commemorate the deliverance of the earth from a giant, who had been a great scourge to the people. He was slain by Vrishnoo, after a dreadful battle. In many places, on this day, a sacrifice is offered to the *dunghill* which is afterwards to enrich the ground. In the villages, each one has his own heap, to which he makes his offering of burning lamps, fruit, flowers, etc.

The most celebrated of all the festivals, is that which is held in the end of December. It is called the feast of Pongul, and is a season of rejoicing for two reasons: the first is, because the month of December, every day of which is unlucky, is about to end; and the other is, because it is to be followed by a month, every day of which is fortunate. For the purpose of preventing the evil effects of this month, the women every morning scour a place about two feet square before the door of the house, upon which they draw white lines, with flour. Upon these they place several little balls of cow-dung, sticking in each a flower. Each day these little balls, with their flowers, are preserved, and on the last day of the month, they are thrown into tanks or waste-places.

The first day of this festival is called the Pongul of rejoicing. Near relatives are invited to a feast, which passes off with mirth and gladness.

The second day is called the Pongul of the sun, and is set apart to worship that luminary. Married women, after bathing themselves, proceed to boil rice with milk, in the open air. When the milk begins to simmer, they make a loud cry, "Pongul, O Pongul." The vessel is then taken from the fire, and set before an idol. Part of this rice is offered to the image, and, after standing there for some time, it is given to the cows. The remainder is given to the people. This is the great day for visiting among friends. The salutation begins by the question, "Has the milk boiled?" To which the answer is, "It has boiled." From this, the festival takes the name of pongul, which signifies to boil.

The third day is called the *Pongul of cows*. In a great vessel, filled with water, they put saffron and other things. These being well mixed, they go around the cows and oxen belonging to the house several times, sprinkling them with water. After this, the men prostrate themselves before them four times. The cows are then dressed, their horns being painted with various colors. Garlands of flowers are also put round their necks, and over their backs. To these are added strings of cocoa-nuts and other kinds of fruit, which, however, are soon shaken off, when they are in motion, and are picked up by children and others, who greedily eat what they gather, as something sacred. After being driven through the streets, they are suffered, during the day, to feed wherever they please, without a keeper. I have, however, told you enough. Are you ready to exclaim, Is it possible that a people can be guilty of such utter folly? But you, my dear children, would be guilty of just such folly, if you had not the Bible. Should not the gratitude, then, which you owe to your heavenly Father, for your distinguished mercies, constrain you to do all that you can to send this blessed book to this dark land?

# CHAPTER XI.

## THE WORSHIP OF THE SERPENT.

My dear Children—If you have never heard much about the Hindoos, you will be astonished to learn how numerous are the objects of their worship. They worship many living creatures, such as the ape, the tiger, the elephant the horse, the ox, the stag, the sheep, the hog, the dog, the cat, the rat, the peacock, the eagle, the cock, the hawk, the serpent, the chameleon, the lizard, the tortoise, fishes, and even insects. Of these, some receive much more worship than others, such as the cow, the ox, and the serpent Cobra Capella. I will speak at present only of the worship of the serpent.

Of all the dangerous creatures found in India, there are none that occasion so many deaths as serpents. The people are very much exposed to their bite, especially at night, when they are walking. They tread upon them, and, as they generally do not wear shoes, the snakes turn their heads, and strike their fangs into those parts of the feet which are nearest to the place where the pressure is made upon their bodies. Sometimes the bite is followed with instant death. The Cobra Capella is one of the most common snakes, and one of the most poisonous. It is said, that it has a thousand heads, one of which holds up the earth. It has a peculiar mark on its back, just behind the head. This mark very much resembles a pair of spectacles, without the handles. If you should go near it, it would raise the fore part of its body about six inches, widen out its neck, so as to be about double its common width, and prepare to strike you. The reason why the Hindoos offer sacrifices and adoration to it above all the other serpents is, because it is so frequently met with, and is so much dreaded.

In order to induce the people to worship this dangerous enemy, the Hindoos have filled their books with tales concerning it. Figures of it are often to be seen in the temples, and on other buildings. They seek out their holes, which are generally to be found in the hillocks of earth which are thrown up by the white ants; and when they find one, they go from time to time and offer milk, plantains, and other good things to it.

The Hindoos, as I before observed, have eighteen annual festivals. One of these festivals is held for the purpose of worshipping this serpent. Temples in many places are erected to it, of which there is one of great celebrity in Mysore. When the festival occurs at this temple, great crowds of people come together to offer sacrifices to this creeping god. Many serpents besides the Cobra Capella live within it, in holes made especially for them. All of these are kept and well fed by the Brahmins with milk, butter, and plantains. By such means they become very numerous, and may be seen swarming from every crevice in the temple. To injure or to kill one would be considered a great crime.

Many of the natives call the Cobra Capella nulla paampu, that is, good snake. They are afraid to call it a bad snake, lest it should injure them. The following is the prayer which is offered before the image of this snake. O, divine Cobra, preserve and sustain us. O, Sheoh, partake of these offerings, and be gracious unto us.

Can you think of any thing, my dear children more dishonoring to a holy God, than such worship? And what have you ever done to prevent it? Have you, every morning and evening, prayed that the Gospel might be sent to this people? Did you ever give any money to send it to them? Did you ever think whether it may not be your duty, by and by, to come to them, to tell them of this Gospel?

# CHAPTER XII.

## THE RIVER GANGES.

My dear Children—If you will look at the map of Asia, and find the country of Hindostan, you will see running through it a very celebrated river—the river Ganges. It is called the Ganges, after the goddess Gunga. The Hindoos say that the goddess Gungu—who was produced from the sweat of Vrishnoo's foot, which Brumha caught and preserved in his alms-dish—came down from heaven, and divided herself into one hundred streams, which are the mouths of the river Ganges. All classes and castes worship her. The sight, the name, or the touch of the river Ganges is said to take away all sin. To die on the edge of the river, or to die partly buried in the stream, drinking its waters, while their bodies are besmeared with mud, is supposed to render them very holy. On this account, when it is expected that a person will die, he is hurried down to the river, whether willing or unwilling. Sometimes the wood which the people bring to burn their bodies after death, is piled up before their eyes. O, how inhuman is this. After it is supposed that they are dead, and they are placed on the pile of wood, if they should revive and attempt to rise, it is thought that they are possessed with the devil, and they are beaten down with a hatchet or bamboo.

Were you standing on the banks of the Ganges you might, perhaps, in one place see two or three young men carrying a sick female to the river. If you should ask what they are going to do with her, perhaps they would reply, We are going to give her up to Gunga, to purify her soul, that she may go to heaven; for she is our mother. In another place you might see a father and mother sprinkling a beloved child with muddy water, endeavoring to soothe his dying agonies by saying, "It is blessed to die by Gunga, my son; to die by Gunga is blessed, my son." In another place you might see a man descending from a boat with empty water-pans tied around his neck, which pans, when filled, will drag down the poor creature to the bottom, to be seen no more. Here is murder in the name of religion. He is a devotee, and has purchased heaven, as he supposes, by this his last good deed. In another place you might see a person seated in the water, accompanied by a priest, who pours down the throat of the dying man mud and water, and cries out, "O mother Gunga, receive his soul." The dying man may be roused to sensibility by the violence. He may entreat his priest to desist; but his entreaties are drowned. He persists in pouring the mud and water down his throat, until he is gradually stifled, suffocated—suffocated in the name of humanity—suffocated in the name of religion.

It happens, sometimes, in cases of sudden and violent attacks of disease, that they cannot be conveyed to the river before death. Under such circumstances, a bone is preserved, and at a convenient season is taken down and thrown into the river. This, it is believed, contributes essentially to the salvation of the deceased.

Sometimes strangers are left on the banks to die, without the ceremony of drinking Ganges water. Of these, some have been seen creeping along with the flesh half eaten off their bones by the birds; others with their limbs torn by dogs and jackals, and others partly covered with insects.

After a person is taken down to the river, if he should recover, it is looked upon by his friends as a great misfortune. He becomes an outcast. Even his own children will not eat with him, nor offer him the least attention. If they should happen to touch him, they must wash their bodies, to cleanse them from the pollution which has been contracted. About fifty miles north of Calcutta, are two villages inhabited entirely by these poor creatures, who have become outcasts in consequence of their recovery after having been taken down to the Ganges.

At the mouth of the river Hoogly, which is one of the branches of the Ganges, is the island Sauger, which I saw as we approached Calcutta after having been at sea for one hundred and twenty-eight days. Now, my dear children, if you come out to India as missionaries, you will have to sail nearly one hundred and thirty days before you can reach it. Sauger island is the island where, formerly, hundreds of mothers were in the habit of throwing their children to the crocodiles, and where these mothers were wont to weep and cry if the crocodiles did not devour their children before their eyes. Think what a dreadful religion that must be, which makes mothers so hard-hearted. Did you ever take any corn or Indian meal and throw it to the chickens? And what did these chickens do? Did they not come around you and eat it? Well, just in this way the crocodiles would come near those mothers, and devour their children. Here is a picture of a mother throwing her child to a crocodile.

    I am glad to tell you, that the British have put a stop to the sacrifice of children at that place; but mothers continue to destroy their children elsewhere, and will continue to destroy them until Christians send the Gospel to them. It is not improbable that vast numbers of children are annually destroyed in the Ganges. Mothers sacrifice them, in consequence of vows which they have made. When the time to sacrifice them has come, they take them down to the river, and encourage them to go out so far that they are taken away by the stream, or they push them off with their own hands.

    I just remarked, that mothers will continue to destroy their children until the Gospel is sent to them. That the Gospel does prevent such things, the following circumstance will show. Several years ago, a missionary lady went from New England to India. As she was walking out one morning, on the banks of the Ganges, she saw a heathen mother weeping. She went up to her, sat down by her side, put her hand into hers, and asked what was the matter with her. "I have just been making a basket of flags," said she, "and putting my infant in it—pushing it off into the river, and drowning it. And my gods are very much pleased with me, because I have done it." After this missionary lady had heard all she had to say, she told her that her gods were no gods; that the only true God delights not in such sacrifices, but turns in horror from them; and that, if she would be happy here and hereafter, she must forsake her sins, and pray to Jesus Christ, who died to save sinners like herself. This conversation was the means of the conversion of that mother, and she never again destroyed any of her infants.

Such is the power of the blessed Gospel. And what the Gospel has done once, it can do again. If Christians will send it to them, with the blessing of God, the time will soon come when heathen mothers will no more destroy their children. And have you nothing to do in this great work, my dear children? When you grow up, cannot you go and tell them of the Saviour? Here is a very pretty hymn about a heathen mother throwing her child to a crocodile.

See that heathen mother stand
Where the sacred currents flow,
With her own maternal hand,'
Mid the waves her infant throw.

Hark, I hear the piteous scream—
Frightful monsters seize their prey,
Or the dark and bloody stream
Bears the struggling child away.

Fainter now, and fainter still,
Breaks the cry upon the ear;
But the mother's heart is steel,
She unmoved that cry can hear.

Send, O send the Bible there,
Let its precepts reach the heart;
She may then her children spare,
Act the mother's tender part.

I have heard of a little boy who learned this hymn. He was deeply affected by it, and wanted very much to give something to send the Gospel to India. But he had no money. He was, however, willing to labor in order to earn some. Hearing that a gentleman wanted the chips removed from the ground near his woodpile, he hired himself to him, removed the chips, got his money, and, with glistening eyes, went and delivered it up, to be sent to the heathen, repeating, as he went,

Send, O send the Bible there,
Let its precepts reach the heart;
She may then her children spare,
Act the mother's tender part.

About one hundred miles above the mouth of the Hoogly is the city of Calcutta, and about five hundred miles above that city is the city of Benares. In these cities, as well as in other places, we see how much the heathen will contribute to support their wretched religion. A rich native in Calcutta has been known to spend more than one hundred thousand dollars on a single festival—the festival of the goddess Karle—and more than thirty thousand dollars every year afterwards during his life, for the same purpose. Not long since, a rich native gave at one time to his idols more than one million two hundred thousand dollars. And what have Christians ever done to honor their Saviour, which will bear a comparison with what the heathen do for their idols? Alas, alas, few Christian men or Christian women, in all the church, are willing to give even one-tenth of their annual income to the Lord. Most of those who are rich, hoard up their money, instead of spending it for the purpose of saving souls. And there are many persons who have never given a farthing to send the Gospel to the heathen. O, what will such say, when they must meet the heathen at the bar of God?

# CHAPTER XIII.

## THE GODDESS DURGA.

My dear Children—From what I said, in my last chapter, about the goddess Gunga, you see that the Hindoos worship goddesses as well as gods. There is another goddess much worshipped the wife of the god Siva. She has appeared in a thousand forms, with a thousand different names. Of all these thousand forms, Durga and Karle are the most regarded by the people. I will speak of Durga first. Of all the festivals in Eastern India, hers is the most celebrated. She has ten hands, in which she holds an iron club, a trident, a battle-axe, spears, thunderbolts, etc. Thus armed, she is ever ready to fight with her enemies.

Were you to be present in the city of Calcutta in the month of September, you might everywhere see the people busy in preparing for the yearly festival of this goddess. Images representing her you would find in great numbers for sale, as bread or meat is sold. In the houses of the rich, images are to be found made of gold, silver, brass, copper, crystal, stone, or mixed metal, which are daily worshipped. These are called permanent images. Besides these, multitudes of what are called temporary images are made—made merely for the occasion and then destroyed. They may be made of hay, sticks, clay, wood, or other such things. Their size varies from a few inches to twenty feet in height. If any persons are too poor to buy one of these images, they can make them for themselves. When the festival is near at hand, people are seen in every direction taking the images to their houses. After they are thus supplied, the festival commences. It lasts fifteen days. The greater part of this time is spent in preparing for the three great days of worship. Early on the morning of the first of the three great days, the Brahmins proceed to consecrate the images, or to give them, as they suppose, life and understanding. Until they are consecrated, they are not thought to be of any value. They are looked upon as senseless. A wealthy family can always receive the services of one or more Brahmins, and a few of the poor may unite and secure the services of one of them. At length the solemn hour arrives. The Brahmin, with the leaves of a sacred tree, comes near the image. With the two forefingers of his right hand he touches the breast, the two cheeks, the eyes, and the forehead of the image, at each touch saying the prayer, "Let the spirit of Durga descend and take possession of this image." By such ceremonies, and by repeating various *muntrums*, it is supposed that the Brahmins have the power to bring down the goddess to take possession of the image. Having been thus consecrated, it is believed to be a proper object of worship. Having eyes, it can now behold every act of worship which is made; having ears, it can be delighted with music and with songs; having a nose, it can smell the sweet perfumes which are offered; having a mouth, it can be delighted with the rich food which is prepared for it.

After the image is consecrated, the worship begins. The devotee comes near the image, and falls down before it. He then twists himself into a great variety of shapes. Sometimes he sits on the floor, sometimes he stands, sometimes he looks in one direction, sometimes in another. Then he sprinkles the idol with holy water, rinses its mouth, washes its feet, wipes it with a dry cloth, throws flowers over it, puts jewels on it, offers perfumes to it, and finishes by performing shaashtaangkum.

The worship of the idol is succeeded by a season of carousing, joy, and festivity. On this occasion, large offerings are made to the idols. A rich native has been known to offer eighty thousand pounds of sweetmeats, eighty thousand pounds of sugar, a thousand suits of cloth garments, a thousand suits of silk, a thousand offerings of rice, plantains, and other fruits.

Bloody sacrifices are offered up on such occasions. The king of Nudiya, some time ago, offered a large number of sheep, goats, and buffaloes on the first day of the feast, and vowed to double the offering every day; so that the whole number sacrificed amounted to more than sixty-five thousand. You may remember that king Solomon offered up on one occasion twenty-two thousand oxen, and a hundred and twenty thousand sheep. If all the animals slain throughout Hindostan, at the festival of the goddess Durga, were collected together, they would amount to a much larger number than Solomon offered.

After the worship and offerings have been continued for three days, the festival closes. As the morning of the first day was devoted to the consecration of the images, the morning of the fourth is spent in unconsecrating them. This work is done by the Brahmins. They profess, by various ceremonies, to send back the goddess to her heaven, concluding with a farewell address, in which they tell her that they expect her to accept of all their services, and return and pay them a visit again in the coming year. Then all unite in bidding her a sorrowful adieu, and many seem affected even to the shedding of tears.

Soon afterwards the images are carried forth into the streets, placed on stages or platforms, and raised on men's shoulders. As the procession moves onward through the streets, accompanied with music and songs, amid clouds of dust, you might see them waving long hairy brushes to wipe off the dust, and to keep off the flies and mosquitoes, which might trouble the senseless images. But where are these processions going? To the banks of the Ganges. And for what purpose? For the purpose of casting the images into the river. When all the ceremonies connected with the occasion are finished, those who carry the images suddenly fall upon them, break them to pieces, and then throw them with violence into the river. After this the people return to their homes.

I have now given you a specimen of the image-worship of the Hindoos; and how different is it from the worship which the Bible enjoins. "God is a Spirit; and they who worship him, must worship him in spirit and in truth." The very reverse of this, as you have seen, marks the worship of the heathen. They are not satisfied, unless they can have some object before them, to which they can make their offerings and their prayers. Thus daily are they engaged in a service which, above all others, is the most offensive and provoking to a holy God—a service which has caused him to declare, that idolaters shall not enter the kingdom of heaven. This, too, is the service in which every person, who has never given himself to the Saviour, is engaged; and, of course, in which you are engaged if you have not given your hearts to him. Those who think more of their money than they think of Christ, just as certainly worship the image which is stamped on a dollar or a cent, as the heathen worship their idols. Those who love their fathers and mothers, and brothers and sisters more than Christ, make these their idols. And are you, my dear children, yet out of Christ? If so, you have your idols. And what are these idols? Are they the world and its vanities? Then God is as angry with you as he is with the heathen, and unless you give up these idols, you too must be lost.

In a tract of mine, published by the American Tract Society, entitled, "Knocking at the Door"—a tract which I *most earnestly* entreat you to get and read—you will find an account of the death of a young lady, who had chosen the world and its vanities as her idols. I was her physician. After having attended her for about a month, I perceived, one morning, that her disease must soon prove fatal. I told her that she could not live. She then exclaimed, "Doctor, can I not live a month?" I informed her that she could not. Again she exclaimed, "Can I not live two weeks?" She was told that she could not live two weeks. And such a scene of horror followed as I never before witnessed, and may God be pleased to grant that I may never witness such another. Until laid upon a dying bed, I fear that she had neglected to think about her soul's concerns. Now she requested to be taken from it, and placed upon her knees, that she might call upon God to have mercy upon her. As her case excited much attention, some of the youth came to see her. These she warned, in the most solemn manner, not to put off repentance, as she had done, to a dying hour. Looking up at me, on one occasion, she exclaimed, "Doctor, cannot you save me?" Alas, what could I do for the poor sufferer. Witness, now, how anxious she was to obtain the favor of that God whom she had hitherto neglected. Yes, so anxious that she requested her friends not to allow her to sleep, that she might spend every remaining breath in calling upon God to have mercy upon her. One very affecting circumstance occurred. She requested her trunk either to be brought to her bedside, or to be opened. From this a ring, which was set with red garnets, was taken out by herself, or by another, and handed to her. She then called a young friend to her bedside, put the ring upon her finger, and said to her, "Don't you put off repentance, as I have done, until a dying hour." That ring is now in my possession. In less than forty-eight hours after I told her that she could not live, she passed into eternity. Would that I could show you that mournful countenance, which continued long after the last spark of life had become extinct; yes, even up to the moment when the lid of her coffin for ever hid it from our view. Never, never shall I forget it. It was a sad monument of the wreck within.

Now, my dear children, you would not like to die as, I fear, this young lady died. Well, then, if you would die differently, you must live differently. You must live for Christ, if you would die in Christ. And are you Christ's, or are you yet gay and thoughtless—as gay and as thoughtless as this young lady was, until laid upon her dying bed? If you are so, and if you continue to remain in this sad condition, your season of sorrow too will certainly come, and it will come when you expect it not. As the little insect which flies round and round your candle is dazzled with its brightness, and feels nothing but pleasure, until it unconsciously strikes the blaze with its little wings, and is swallowed up in the flame; so you are dazzled with the pleasures of the world, thinking nothing of the flames which may swallow you up in a moment, and put a stop to all your joys for ever. O, that the death-bed scene of Miss Matthews might have a happy effect upon you. O, that the solemn warning which she gave to her young friend, not to put off repentance as she had done, until a dying hour, might continue to sound in your ears, until you would no longer delay repentance. My dear children, this young lady, though dead, yet speaketh. She speaks to you. She calls upon you from her tomb—from the eternal world, to delay repentance no longer. Will you, then, be so mad as to turn a deaf ear to this call? Will you ever take another sip from the cup of unhallowed pleasure? Will you ever direct your little feet to the ballroom, or other places of sinful amusement? Will you hereafter prefer your worldly joys to Christ? O, you must not, you must not. It will not do for you to be lost. Who, O who can lie down in everlasting burnings? Who can dwell for ever with devouring flames?

# CHAPTER XIV.

## THE GODDESS KARLE.

My dear Children—In the preceding chapter I spoke of Karle. She, as I there mentioned, is the wife of Siva, and, like her husband, has the power of destruction. From the images made of her, it would appear that she is a female, of a black or dark blue color. She has four arms. In one hand she holds a sword, and in another a human head. Her hair is dishevelled, reaching down to her feet. Her countenance is most ferocious. Her tongue comes out of her mouth, and hangs over her chin. She has three eyes, red and fiery. Her lips and eyebrows are streaked with blood. She has two dead bodies for ear-rings, and wears a girdle around her loins—a girdle made of bloody hands, which she cut off from the bodies of her enemies. She has a necklace of skulls, which she took from the bodies of the giants and others killed by her.

Of all the Hindoo divinities, this goddess is the most cruel and revengeful. Such is her thirst for blood, that being unable at one time to procure any giants for her prey, in order to quench her thirst, she cut her own throat, that the blood issuing thence might spout into her mouth. Different acts of worship are performed to appease her. If, for example, a devotee should burn his body, by applying a burning lamp to it, it would be very pleasing to her. If he should draw some of his blood and give it to her, or if he should cut off a piece of his flesh and offer it as a burnt-offering, she would be still move pleased. If he should present *whole* burnt-offerings upon the altar, saying, "Hrang, brang, Karle, Karle! O, horrid-toothed goddess, eat, eat; destroy all the malignant: cut with this axe; bind, bind; seize, seize; drink this blood; spheng, spheng; secure, secure; salutation to Karle," she would be much delighted. It is said that she will be pleased for three months, if the people offer her the blood of a crocodile—for a thousand years, if they offer her the blood of one man, and a hundred thousand years, if they offer her the blood of three.

This goddess is the patroness of thieves. To her they pay their devotions, to obtain help to carry on their wicked delights. Gangs meet together, and, after having offered bloody sacrifices, and worshipped their weapons, and having drunk some intoxicating liquor, and rubbed their bodies with oil, they go forth to rob. They have a prayer, which they offer when they worship their weapons. It is as follows: "O, instrument formed by the goddess, Karle commands thee to cut a passage into the house, to cut through stones, bones, bricks, wood, the earth, and mountains, and cause the dust thereof to be carried away by the wind." Scattered throughout India, there is a lawless set of men whose profession it is to get their food by murder. They are called Phansiagars, or Thugs. They owe their origin and laws to Karle. They say that she told them to become murderers and plunderers. They are called Phansiagars, from the name of the instrument which they use when they murder people. Phansiagar means a strangler, and they use a phansi, or noose, which they throw over the necks of those whom they intend to plunder, and strangle them. These Phansiagars are composed of all castes, Hindoos, Mahommedans, pariahs, and chandellars. This arises from the circumstance that they never destroy the children of those whom they rob and murder. These children they take care of, and bring up to their own horrible mode of life. They always murder those whom they rob, acting upon the maxim that "dead men tell no tales." A gang of these robbers varies from a dozen to sixty or seventy persons. These divide into small parties. Those whom they murder are travellers, whom they happen to meet on the road. Sometimes two or three of a gang will take up their station in a choultry, or place where the traveller stops, and while he sleeps, they rouse him from his sleep, and cast the noose over his head and kill him. It takes two persons to kill a man. One casts the noose over his head, and immediately tightens it with all his strength; the other strikes him on the joint of his knees as he rises, which causes him to fall forwards. After he has fallen, they kick him on the temples till he dies, which is usually in a minute. They never commit a murder until they have taken every precaution not to be found out. They will follow a traveller for weeks, if necessary, before they destroy him. After they have murdered him, they gash the body all over and bury it. They gash it, that it may not swell, and cause cracks to take place in the ground, which might cause the jackals to dig down to the body, and thus expose their guilt. If a dog accompanies the person, they always kill it, lest the faithful creature should lead to the discovery of his master. They think it to be a very good act to give a part of the plunder, which they get when they murder a person, to their goddess. If they fail to put him to death according to their rules, they suppose that they have made her angry, and they make offerings to her, that she may be appeased. Thus, you see that their religion teaches them to commit the blackest of crimes.

The reason why this people gash and bury the bodies of those whom they murder, is as follows. They say that the goddess used to save them the trouble of burying the corpses of their victims by eating them, thus screening the murderers from all chance of being found out. Once, after the murder of a traveller, the body was, as usual, left unburied. One of the Phansiagars employed, unguardedly looking behind him, saw the goddess in the act of feasting upon it. This made her so angry, that she vowed never again to devour a body slaughtered by them; they having, by this one act of curiosity, forfeited her favor. However, as an equivalent for withdrawing her patronage, she plucked one of the fangs from her jaw, and gave it to them, saying that they might use it as a pickaxe, which would never wear out. She then opened her side and pulled out one of her ribs, which she gave them for a knife, whose edge nothing could blunt. Having done this, she stooped down and tore off the hem of her garment, which she gave to them for a noose, declaring that it would never fail to strangle any person about whose throat it might be cast. She moreover commanded them to gash and bury the bodies of those whom they destroyed.

The Phansiagars bring up their children to their own profession. To learn this, the boy is placed under the care of a tutor. Sometimes his father is his teacher. By him he is taught that it is just as proper to murder a man, as it is to kill a snake which lies in his path and would bite him as he passes. He is not permitted at first to see the murders, but merely a dead body; his mind being gradually prepared for the sight. After this, the dreadful secret of his trade is, by degrees, told him. When he expresses a wish to be engaged in this horrid business, they tell him all about it. In the meantime he is allowed a small part of the plunder, in order that his desire to commit these murders may be increased; since it is only by murder that the plunder is obtained. He is from time to time allowed to assist in some things, while the murder is taking place, or allowed to be present to see how the business is managed. It is not, however, until he becomes a man, that he is permitted to apply the noose. To attain this privilege, he usually devotes eight or ten years. Before he can commit a murder, his tutor must present him with a noose. This sets him loose upon the world, as a licensed murderer. When the tutor is about to give him the noose, he takes him apart, and solemnly enjoins it upon him to use it with skill, as it is to be the means of his earning his food, and as his safety will depend upon the skill with which it is used. After he receives it, he tries his skill in strangling a person the first opportunity that offers.

By the course of education which the Phansiagars undergo, they become so fond of their dreadful occupation, that nothing can induce them to quit it. Some who have been employed in the East India Company's service, have always returned to their business when an opportunity offered of a successful enterprise.

When the Phansiagars become old, they do not quit the service, but act as watchers, and decoy the traveller, by some false tale of distress, into some distant place, where he is murdered.

Women are sometimes admitted to the society of these plunderers, and, on some occasions, are allowed to apply the noose. They select a handsome girl, and place her in a convenient spot, where, by her beauty, or by a false story of distress, she may decoy some unsuspecting traveller, and be the means of his destruction. Should he be on horseback, she will induce him to take her up behind him; after which, when an opportunity offers, she throws the noose over his head, leaps from the horse, drags him to the ground, and strangles him. I will mention an instance. It happened that a horseman of Coorg, in the Madras presidency, was passing by a spot where one of these interesting-looking girls was stationed. She told him a piteous story of having been robbed and badly treated, and begged him to assist her. Feeling sorry for her, he offered to take her behind him, on his horse, and thus assist her a few miles on her journey. She expressed much gratitude for his kindness, and mounted. Soon afterwards she suddenly passed a noose over his head, and, drawing it with all her might, endeavored to pull him from his saddle. At this moment, a number of Phansiagars started from the neighboring thicket and surrounded him. The murderess then slipped from the horse; but the Coorg striking his heels into the horse's sides, it threw out its hind legs with great violence, and struck to the ground the girl, who immediately let go the cord. He then drew his sword, and, cutting his way through the robbers, effected his escape. He wounded two of them severely. These men were shortly afterwards taken, and, through their means, twelve others fell into the hands of the judicial officers of the king of Coorg, including the girl who attempted the murder. They were all put to death.

And is it possible that such persons can go to heaven? How could such ever relish its pure joys? What would they do, could they be admitted there? My dear children, it is a charity which has no foundation, to suppose that the heathen can go to heaven. I have preached the Gospel to tens of thousands of them, but I never saw one who had the least atom of a qualification for that holy place. "They have all gone out of the way." Every crime which the apostle Paul speaks of in the latter part of the first chapter of his epistle to the Romans, they commit, and crimes of so dreadful a nature that I cannot mention them—crimes which, should they be written in the Bible, would cause the Bible to be a sealed book for ever.

# CHAPTER XV.

## SELF-TORTURES OF THE HINDOOS.

My dear Children—As the heathen have no Bible to direct them, they have devised various means by which they expect to obtain the favor of their gods, and get to heaven. I will mention some of these.

Some burn a lamp in a temple. They think that this is a very meritorious act. Some roll on the ground after the god, as he is carried in a great car or chariot around the temple. It is customary for the people to build very high cars or chariots, and cover them with very beautiful cloths. They also tie the cocoa-nut blossom and plantain-tree within them, and attach great ropes to them. When they are ready to drag these cars, or chariots, they bring their gods of gold or of brass from the temples, and place them on them. Then one, two, three, six, nine hundred, and even a thousand persons, when the cars are very large, catch hold of these ropes and drag them around the temple. While they are doing this, many of the heathen, to fulfil vows which they made when in sickness, and at other times of distress, throw themselves on the ground, and roll over from side to side, and frequently much injure themselves.

Some swing on great hooks, which are passed through the tender parts of their backs. Sometimes they swing for half an hour; sometimes an hour. The longer they can bear the torture of the swinging, the more acceptable they suppose it will be to their goddess. It occasionally happens, that the flesh in which the hooks are fastened gives way, in which case the poor creature is dashed to the ground. When this occurs, the people hold him in the greatest abhorrence. They judge him to be a great criminal, and suppose that he has met a violent death in consequence of sins which he committed in a former birth.

Not long since, I attended one of these hook-swingings, not far from the city of Madura. It took place on the morning of June 8th, 1848, just twenty-nine years after I first left America for India. It should have taken place on the preceding afternoon; but one of the axle-trees of the car, which was to support the machine on which the man was to be elevated in the air, was broken. Nothing, of course, could be done until it was repaired. The carpenters and others worked with great diligence until about eleven o'clock at night, when every thing was prepared for the swinging. I expected immediately after this to witness the ceremony. It however did not take place until the morning. While waiting for the man who was to be swung to make his appearance, I took a pencil and made a drawing of the machine to which he was to be fastened. The picture on the first page of the book will give you some idea of it.

Yon have, perhaps, often seen a well-sweep. The long beam in the picture is swung in the same manner as is the well-sweep, with a single exception. In addition to its usual motion, it is made to turn horizontally. The cuts which you may have seen, in two or three of my little books, differ much from the above; of course different machines are used at different times. There are stationary swingings, as well as swingings of the kind to which I just alluded.

Between six and seven o'clock in the morning, the man who was to be swung made his appearance for a few moments, and then disappeared. The hooks by which he was to be swung, as well as the iron rods with which a number of devotees were immediately to pierce their sides, were carried through the streets, and held up that they might be seen by the people. Soon afterwards the man again appeared with the hooks in his back, and went up to the end of the beam to which he was to be fastened. This, of course, was lowered. Notwithstanding the dense multitudes of people, I made my way to the same spot, determined to be satisfied whether or not there was any deception in the application of the hooks. There was no deception. They passed through the skin, on the sides of the backbone. To these hooks were attached yellow ropes, by which he was fastened to the beam, as you will perceive in the picture. This being done, the men, five or six in number, who had hold of the ropes fastened to the end of the beam which you see resting on the ground, and which was then, of course, high in the air, drew him up until the beam lay horizontally. Then, after making him perform one circular motion around the car, they elevated him, as you see in the picture. When thus elevated, it was thought that he was forty feet from the ground. All being ready, the people seized the ropes which you see in front of the car, and began to draw it. Mr. Chandler and myself accompanied it through the streets, until it came to the place from which it set out. The distance of ground passed over was at least half a mile, and the time in which the journey was accomplished exceeded an hour. Of course he was swinging more than an hour. As the car passed through the streets, the people threw plantains from the tops of the houses to the crowds below.

The man who was swung was adorned with flowers and other ornaments. He had a tinselled turban on his head. His body was rubbed over with a yellow paste, made, most probably, from the sandal-wood. Around his ankles were rings, hung with little bells, which he made to tinkle, as he was swinging, by striking his legs together. He wore a dark or black pair of pantaloons, which came a little below the knees, and which had a border of gold around them. He held a handkerchief in one hand, and a knife somewhat resembling a dagger, in the other. These he kept in constant motion, by moving his arms. On one occasion, a bunch of plantains was tied to one of the long ropes which you see hanging down by the side of the swinger. These he drew up, and afterwards scattered over the people on a house opposite to him.

After following the car for a quarter of a mile or more, we went before it, and there witnessed another appalling sight. There were five or six men, who had the rods of iron which I just mentioned passed through the skin of their sides. They were dancing along, and, as they danced, they made these rods go backward and forward through the skin.

After the car had reached the place from which it set out, the end of the beam from which the man was swinging was then lowered and he was untied. Again I looked very carefully at the hooks in the back. The people say that no blood is shed by their introduction, and consider this to be a miracle. The falsity of this assertion was shown by the blood which I saw on the side of one of the wounds.

I have been long in this country, and consequently have become so familiarized with heathenism, that my feelings, though deeply wounded at this sight, were not so keenly affected as were those of my new associate, Mr. Chandler. He has been on heathen ground but a short time. When they tied the man to the beam, he was unnerved and wellnigh overcome; and he told me, that during all the time he was following the car, he felt like shedding tears.

While following the car, the young men of America came into my mind. They refuse to come, said I, to help these miserable creatures. O, they will not come—they will not come. I thought, that if many of the dear children of that land—children to whom I lately preached, as well as others, could witness this poor creature swinging from the end of a long beam, far above the tops of the trees, and that, too, by hooks passing through the tender parts of his back, they would say, we will, by and by, become missionaries, and, by the help of God, proclaim to the heathen that there is a Saviour.

On the evening of the day on which the swinging takes place, another act of great cruelty is practised. Devotees throw themselves from, the top of a high wall, or a scaffold of twenty or thirty feet in height, upon a bed of iron spikes, or on bags of straw with knives in them. Many are often mangled and torn. Others are quickly killed.

At night, many of the devotees sit down in the open air, and pierce the skin of their foreheads, by inserting a small rod of iron. To this is suspended a lamp, which is kept burning till daylight.

Sometimes bundles of thorns are collected before the temple, among which the devotees roll themselves without any covering. These thorns are then set on fire, when they briskly dance over the flames.

Other devotees swing before a slow fire; some stand between two fires, as you see in this picture.

Some have their breasts, arms, and other parts stuck entirely full of pins, about the thickness of small nails, or packing needles.

Another very cruel torture is practised. Some of the devotees make a vow. With one hand they cover their under lip with wet earth or mud. On this, with the other hand, they place some small grains, usually of mustard-seed They then stretch themselves flat on their backs, exposed to the dews of night, and the blazing and scorching sun by day. Their vow is, that from this position they will not stir, that they will not move nor turn, nor eat nor drink, till the seeds planted on their lips begin to sprout. This usually takes place on the third or fourth day. After this they arise, and then think that they are very holy.

There is a class of devotees in this country called Yogis, whose object it is to root out every human feeling. Some live in holes and caves. Some drag around a heavy chain attached to them. Some make the circuit of an empire, creeping on their hands and knees. Some roll their bodies from the shores of the Indus to the Ganges.

The Rev. Mr. Heyer, in one of his letters from India, says, that an Indian devotee has spent more than nine years on a journey from Benares to Cape Comorin, that is, from the 27th to the 7th degree of north latitude. The whole journey is made by rolling on the bare ground, from side to side. When he comes to a river, of course he cannot roll over it. He therefore fords it, or passes over it in a boat, and then rolls on the banks of the river just as far as the river is wide. By doing this, he supposes that his determination to roll all the way is fully carried out.

Some devotees hold up one or both arms, until the muscles become rigid, and their limbs become shrivelled into stumps. In the above cut, you have a representation of a man with one of these shrivelled arms. See how long his finger-nails have grown. One has run through his hand and back through his arm. Some stretch themselves on beds of iron spikes. Some wear great square irons on their necks. I have seen not only a man, but a woman, with these great square irons around their necks, each nearly two feet in length and two feet in breadth. These they put on for the purpose of fulfilling some vow which they have made. For instance, if a mother has a very sick little boy, she will say, "Now, Swammie, if you will cure my little boy, I will have a square iron put on my neck, and wear it all my life." After this vow is made, if the little boy gets well, the mother thinks that her Swammie has cured him, and to fulfil her engagement she will have one of these irons put on her neck.

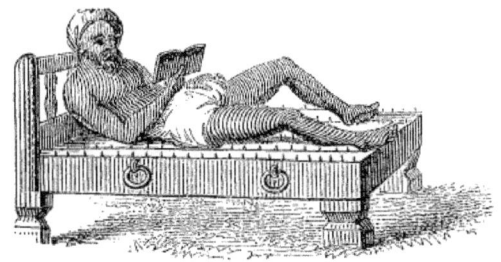

Other devotees throw themselves from the tops of precipices, and are dashed to pieces; some bury themselves alive in holes, which their own relatives have dug; some bind themselves with ropes or chains to trees, until they die; some keep gazing so long and so constantly at the heavens, that the muscles of their neck become contracted, and no aliment but liquids can pass into the stomach.

But I will not continue this subject. You perceive, my dear children, what a wretched religion that must be which encourages its followers to perform such acts. And how vain are all these acts—how utterly destitute are they of any merit. Those who practise them are not made better by them, and they are just as far from the kingdom of heaven after having performed them, as they were before. The Christian religion encourages no such things. It tells us to perform no pilgrimages to holy places, to inflict no self-tortures. But it has its requirements, and these are very simple, and may easily be performed by all who are willing to do their duty. These requirements are, repentance, forsaking sin, faith in Christ, and a supreme devotedness to his service. Have you, my dear children, attended to these requirements? If not, you are in a much worse condition than these poor heathen of whom you have been reading. They are not as guilty before God as you are. They know not their Master's will. Still, they must perish, unless the Gospel is sent to them. But though they perish, their punishment will be lighter than the punishment of those who refuse to love and obey the Saviour. That servant who knows his Lord's will, and prepares not himself, neither does according to his will, shall be beaten with many stripes. But he that knows not, and does commit things worthy of stripes, shall be beaten with few stripes. Should it be your sad lot to perish at last, it would be far better for you to go down to hell enveloped in all the darkness of a heathen land, than to go down to hell from a land of such gospel light and privileges as you enjoy.

# CHAPTER XVI.

## THE SUTTEE, OR BURNING OF WIDOWS.

My dear children—From what I have already told you, you know that the Hindoos are a cruel people. But I have not told you of the extent to which they carry their cruelty. Perhaps it is shown to the highest degree in their practice of the suttee, or burning of widows. The British have abolished this rite throughout their dominions in India. They have also made great exertions to have it abolished in the territories of the native princes, but I am sorry to say, that in some of these territories it is still practised. Within the last three years, twenty-three of the princes just alluded to, have issued orders for its abolishment throughout their dominions. These orders have probably been issued solely in consequence of their fear of the British power, for it is a practice which is riveted in the affections of the people. This power they know that it will be dangerous to resist.

In my "Sermon to Children, on the Condition of the Heathen," I mentioned, that the sacred books of the heathen encourage the suttee. I also mentioned several instances, in which widows had been burned to death with the corpses of their husbands. Even though you may have seen that book, it will be well for me to give you two or three other cases, to impress your minds more fully with the horrors of the Hindoo religion. The first took place in a village of Tanjore. A merchant having died, his wife, who was about thirty years old, determined to burn herself with his corpse. The news of what she was going to do, quickly spread in every direction, and large numbers of people collected to witness the burning. After she was adorned with jewels and dressed in her best clothing, and after her body was tinged with the yellow infusion of sandal-wood and saffron, bearers arrived to take away the corpse with the wretched woman. The body of the man was placed on a car, ornamented with costly stuffs, flowers, etc. There he was seated like a living man, elegantly decorated with all his jewels, and clothed in rich attire.

The corpse being carried first, the wife followed in a rich palanquin. As she went along, the surrounding multitudes of people stretched out their hands towards her to show how much they admired her conduct. The women in particular went up to her to wish her joy, apparently desiring to receive her blessing, or at least, that she would pronounce over them some pleasing word. She tried to satisfy them all, saying to one, that she would long continue to enjoy her worldly happiness, and to another, that she would be the mother of many beautiful children. Another was informed, that she would soon arrive at great honor in the world. These, and similar expressions, she made to all who came near her, and they departed with the full belief that they would enjoy all the blessings of which she had spoken. She also distributed among them some betel-leaves, which they gladly received as relics, or something of blessed influence.

During the whole procession, which was very long, her countenance was serene and even cheerful, until they came to the pile upon which she was to die. Then she suddenly became pensive. She no longer attended to what was passing around her. Her looks were wildly fixed upon the pile. Her face grew pale. She trembled with fear, and seemed ready to faint away.

The Brahmins, who took the lead in this ceremony, with her relations, seeing her sad condition, ran to her, and endeavored to restore her spirits, but she seemed not to know what they said, and answered not a word.

They made her quit the palanquin, and her nearest relatives took her to a pond of water which was near the pile, where they washed her. They then attended her to the pile, on which the corpse of her husband had already been laid. It was surrounded with Brahmins, each with a lighted torch in one hand, and a bowl of melted butter in the other, all ready, as soon as the poor victim was placed on the pile, to envelope her in fire.

The relatives armed with muskets, sabres, and other weapons, stood closely around in a double line, for the purpose, it was said, of making her afraid, if she might wish to draw back, or of frightening any body who might pity her, and endeavor to rescue her.

At length the time for firing the pile being proclaimed, the young widow was stripped of her jewels, and led on towards the pile. She was then commanded to walk three times around it, two of her nearest relations supporting her by the arms. The first round she accomplished with tottering steps; but in the second, her strength forsook her, and she fainted away in the arms of those who were holding her. They were obliged to drag her between them for the third round. Then senseless, she was thrown upon the corpse of her husband. At that instant, the multitude made the air to ring with their shouts of gladness, while the Brahmins poured the butter on the dry wood, and applied the torches. Instantly the whole pile was in a blaze.

As soon as the flames began to rage, the poor woman, now in the midst of them, was called upon by name, from all sides; but as insensible as the corpse on which she lay, she made no answer. She entered eternity, suffocated at once, most probably, by the flames.

The second case of suttee which I shall mention took place at the death of the rajah, or king of Tanjore. He left behind him four wives.

The Brahmins having determined that two of these four should be burned with the corpse of their husband, and having selected the two whom they thought best to sacrifice, they told them of what awaited them. They received the information with apparent joy. A refusal would have been attended with their utter disgrace.

One day only was necessary to get ready for the funeral ceremonies. They were conducted as follows: In a field somewhat distant from the palace, the people made a hollow, not very deep, but about twelve or fifteen feet square. Within it they made a pyramid of the sweet-smelling sandal-wood. On the middle of the pyramid, a scaffold was built in such a manner that the posts could easily be taken away, by which means the scaffold would fall at once. On the four corners of the platform, large jars were placed, filled with melted butter, to besmear the pyramid, that it might be the more easily set on fire.

The following was the order of the procession. It was headed by a great number of soldiers under arms. They were followed by a multitude of musicians, chiefly trumpeters, who made the air reëcho with their melancholy sounds. Next came the body of the king upon a splendid palanquin, richly adorned. This was surrounded by the nearest relations and by the priest of the king. They were all on foot, and without their turbans in token of mourning. A large party of Brahmins formed around them as an immediate escort. The two wives who were to be burned with the corpse came next, each borne on a palanquin. During the journey they appeared calm and cheerful. The troops kept off the immense crowds who were assembled from every direction.

The two queens, loaded with jewels, were attended by their favorite women, with whom they occasionally conversed, and by their relations of both sexes. To many of these they had made presents before leaving the palace. They were also accompanied by thousands of Brahmins, collected from different quarters. These were followed by an innumerable multitude of persons of both sexes. When they arrived at the ground where they were to be burned, the two victims were made to descend from their palanquins, for the purpose of performing the preparatory ceremonies. They went through the whole without showing any fear until towards the close, when their countenances began to change, and their three circuits around the pile were not performed without considerable effort to maintain calmness.

In the meantime, the body of the king had been placed on the scaffold over the platform. The two queens were also laid down beside the corpse, one on the right hand, and the other on the left, and they joined hands by stretching them over the body. The astrologer having then declared that the happy moment was come for firing the pile, the Brahmins repeated several prayers in a loud voice, and sprinkled the pile with holy water. When these ceremonies were finished, a signal was given, and the pillars which supported the pyramid and the scaffold were suddenly taken away. Immediately the women were covered with the falling mass of timber, which tumbled over them with a crash. At the same instant the pile was fired in all its parts. On one side, the nearest relative of the king applied his torch, and on the other side, the priest; while the Brahmins, in every quarter, were pouring jars of melted butter on the flames, creating so intense a heat as must instantly have consumed the victims. Then the multitude shouted for joy, and the relations approaching the pile also set up a loud cry, calling them by their names. They supposed that they heard a voice in answer pronouncing *Enna?* that is, *What?* but the fall of the platform, and the immediate bursting out of the flames, must have stifled them at once.

Such was the miserable cud of these poor unhappy queens—unhappy victims of the most cruel religion that ever disgraced the earth.

Not unfrequently the sons take a prominent part in destroying their mothers. This will appear from the following case. A Brahmin died, and was brought to the place of burning. His wife was fastened to the pile, and the fire was kindled, but the night was dark and rainy. When the fire began to scorch the poor woman, she contrived to disentangle herself from the dead body, and creeping from under the pile, hid herself among some brushwood. In a little time it was discovered that there was but one body on the pile. The relations immediately took the alarm, and searched for the poor creature. The son soon dragged her forth, and insisted that she should throw herself on the pile again, or drown or hang herself. She pleaded for her life at the hands of her own son, and declared that she could not embrace so horrid a death; but she pleaded in vain. He urged, that he should lose his caste if she were spared, and added, that either he or she must die. Unable to persuade her to hang or drown herself, the son and the others present tied her hands and feet, and threw her on the funeral pile, where she quickly perished.

I observed that the rite of suttee is riveted in the affections of this people. The following communications from two of the native princes who lately consented to put a stop to this rite, will show you that this is the case. The rajah of Oorcha declares, that "no subject of his state shall in future be permitted to become a suttee, though according to the Shasters, it is no doubt very meritorious for a widow to die of grief for the death of her husband." The rajah of Sumpthem says, "The practice of suttee is so very old, and has been countenanced and encouraged by the wise men of so many generations that I have never thought myself justified in interposing to prevent it; but my anxiety to meet the wishes of the governor-general in this and in all things, is so great, that I have waived all other considerations, and forbidden suttee."

If the British were to lose their power in India, the suttee would immediately be reëstablished. Power has put it down, but power alone will never root it out of the affections of the people. Nothing but the Gospel can do this. O that Christians would think of this, and hasten, yea, with great haste, to send this blessed Gospel to them.

# CHAPTER XVII.

## THE REVENGEFUL NATURE OF THE HINDOO RELIGION.

My dear Children—The sacred books of the Hindoos encourage revenge. In the Vedas, which are the most sacred books, are laid down forms of religious service, or acts of worship, which are designed to injure or destroy their enemies. When a person wishes to have his enemy destroyed, he goes to a Brahmin or priest, and secures his supposed aid. The Brahmin, before he proceeds to his work, clothes himself with a black garment. He also makes four images of the foe, and clothes these with black garments. He then kindles a sacrificial fire, and after the performance of various ceremonies, he takes pieces of some animal which has been consecrated for the purpose, and throws them into this fire. On every occasion when he makes this burnt-offering, he touches the mouth of the image of this enemy, uttering one or other of the forms of prayer which are written in the sacred books. Of these, the following are a few: "O Agni," god of fire, "thou who art the mouth of all gods, do thou destroy the wisdom of my enemy." "O Agni, fill with distraction the mind of this my enemy." "O Agni, destroy the senses of this my enemy." "O Agni, make dumb the mouth of this my enemy." "O Agni, fasten with a peg the tongue of this my enemy." "O Agni, reduce to ashes this my enemy."

How different, my dear children, is the religion of Jesus from the religion of which I have been giving you a description. No precepts teach us that we may injure or destroy our enemies. On the contrary, they teach us to love them, and do them good. Let me repeat to you some of the words which our Saviour spoke on this point. "Ye have heard that it hath been said, Thou shalt love thy neighbor, and hate thine enemy; but I say unto you, love your enemies, bless them that curse you, do good to them that hate you, and pray for them that despitefully use you and persecute you, that ye may be the children of your Father which is in heaven; for he maketh his sun to rise on the evil and on the good, and sendeth rain on the just and on the unjust."

One of the young Hindoos in Dr. Duff's school in Calcutta, when reading the above and similar passages, was so struck with the difference between these precepts and the precepts of his Shasters, that he could not but exclaim "O, how beautiful, how divine. Surely this is the truth—this is the truth—this is the truth." The consequence was, that he never could rest until he had thrown aside his sacred books and his idols, and embraced that Saviour whose precepts appeared to him to be so beautiful. And was this heathen so struck with the beauty of the precepts of the Bible—so struck, that he had no peace until he gave himself to his Saviour? And have you ever, my dear children, been struck with the precepts of your Saviour—so struck with them, that you could never rest until you had given up your hearts to him? If not, how great is the contrast between you and that young Hindoo. He gave his heart to the Saviour. You withhold yours. He, through grace, will dwell for ever with Christ in heaven. You, if you continue in your present awful condition, must be banished from his presence, and cast into hell, where you shall be tormented day and night for ever, with the devil and his angels. Flee, my dear children, flee to the Saviour now, if you have never yet done so. Flee to him, and then you also shall dwell for ever with him.

# CHAPTER XVIII.

## THE DECEPTION OF THE HINDOOS.

My dear Children—From what I have previously stated, you are aware that the Hindoos are a very deceitful people. Let me give you another instance of their deception. A late head catechist of one of my missionary brethren was, before his conversion, the priest of a temple. A man from whom about one thousand rupees' worth of jewels and similar things had been stolen, came to this priest, and promised to reward him well, if he would detect the thief, and secure to him the restoration of his property. The priest promised to comply with his wishes; and in order to effect his purpose, he had drums beaten through the village, and proclaimed, that at a certain time he would hold a meeting and detect the thief. At the appointed time, a large concourse of people assembled, the priest appearing in the midst of them with a cocoa-nut bound around with saffron-cords. He then told them, that if, after putting down the cocoa-nut, it should move of its own accord towards him, they might know that he would be able certainly to detect the thief; and added, that after it had thus moved, it would pursue the offender, and follow him until it would break his head. He then performed certain ceremonies calculated to awaken superstitious feelings in the minds of the people, and laid the cocoa-nut down at a little distance from him. To the great amazement of all present, it began to move towards the priest, and continued to move until it reached his feet. This being done, he told the people, that they might conclude from what they had seen, that the cocoa-nut would follow the thief until it would break his head. He consented, however, to give him a little grace—to spare his life until the next day; adding his advice, that the thief, whoever he might be, had better come to him privately, and tell him where the property was. In the dead of the night, a tap was heard at the door of the priest; the thief presented himself, and delivered up the property. The priest received a present from the owner of the property, and rewarded the thief for his promptness. After this man was converted, he was asked how he contrived to make the cocoa-nut move towards him. "Why, sir," he answered, "if you will carefully divide a cocoa-nut, scoop out the kernel from one-half of it, enclose a strong, lively rat, put the parts of the cocoa-nut together, and bind the whole with saffron-cords, to prevent the crack being seen, and then place it on a declivity previously prepared, it is clear, that if you place yourself at the foot of this declivity the rat will twirl the cocoa-nut, and cause it to descend until it reaches your feet."

# CHAPTER XIX.

## SUPERSTITION OF THE HINDOOS.

My dear Children—In my Sermon to Children, before alluded to, I mentioned a few particulars to prove that the people of India are very superstitious. Let me mention a few more. It is said that no act, however good it may be, if performed on Sunday, will succeed. Some will not eat at all on Sunday, until they have seen a certain bird—the bird on which the god Vrishnoo rides. If a man rubs oil on his head on Monday, and bathes, he will commit a sin equal to the sin of destroying a temple of Siva. If he has his hair out on Tuesday, he will become poor. Even to worship the gods on Wednesday, is bad. If a person takes medicine on Thursday, his sickness will be increased. Should he lend any thing on Friday, he will lose his property. If he should buy a new cloth on Saturday, take it home, and keep it there, death may be the consequence. Should he die on this day, some other member of the family will die on the following week.

If the foundation of a house is laid in June, the destruction of that house will follow. Should a family enter a new house in March, some member of the family will die. If a marriage is celebrated in September, the husband and wife will fight with each other.

Should a thunderbolt fall on a house, or a vulture alight on it, some evil will befall the people living in it. If a crow should strike any person on the head with its wings, some of his relations will die. Should a cat or a snake cross his path, it would be an indication of evil. In the latter case, one of his relations will die. If, when returning home, a person should meet him bearing a light, a quarrel will be the result.

After a person has left his house, should he meet a single Brahmin, or a woman who has had her head shaved, or a dumb or a blind man, or a washerman or a barber, the object for which he left would not succeed. Or, when going out, should he hit his head against the top of the door-frame, or should any one ask him where he was going, or should he happen to sneeze, he would consider these things as hinderances to his going, and reënter the house.

Should a son or a daughter be born on the new moon in April, they will become thieves. If a person is born under the planet Saturn, he will be slandered, his riches will be dissipated, and his wife, son, and friends will be destroyed. He will also be at variance with others, and endure many sufferings. Should he be born under the planet Mars, he will be full of anxious thoughts, be imprisoned, and oppressed with fear from robbers, fire, etc. He also will lose his lands, trees, and good name.

If a person dreams that a monkey has bitten him, he will die in six months; or if he dreams that bedbugs, in large numbers, are creeping over his body to bite him, he will die in eight days. Should he dream that a dog has bitten him, he will die in three years; or should he dream that a dead person has appeared to him and spoken to him, he will die immediately.

If a man has a little head, he will become rich. If he has a large head, he will be poor. If his forehead is wide, he will live a hundred years. If he has a small neck, he will be a murderer. If the second toe is long, he will be a bad man. If a woman has curly hair, she will not prosper. If her nose is long, she will have a good disposition. If her ear is wide, she will tell falsehoods. If she has a mole on her nose, she will be subject to anger; if on her lips, she will be learned; if on the eyebrows she will be cunning.

I could continue to fill a number of pages with things of the same description, but it will be unnecessary. I will merely mention one instance more. On a certain night in the month of November, the people will not look at the moon. The reason assigned for this, is as follows. Once, when the elephant-faced god Pulliar was dancing before the gods, the moon happening to see him, laughed at him, and told him that he had a large stomach, an ear like a winnowing-fan, etc. This so enraged him, that he cursed her. This curse was inflicted on the night above mentioned.

How does the wretchedness of a people, both in reference to the things of this world and of the world to come, show itself where the Bible is unknown. If this blessed book was not an inspired book—if it did no more than remove the temporal miseries of men, how invaluable would it be! Of how much more value then, is it, in reference to the removal of their spiritual miseries?

O, why is it that Christians have not long since sent this Bible to them? Why is it that they do not send it to them *now*? This is a mystery, which we must leave to be unravelled at the judgment-seat of the last day. My dear children, you are to stand before that judgment-seat. Shall any of these heathen among whom I dwell, rise up at that awful season—stretch out their hands towards you, and say, There stand the children who might have sent us the Bible, but they did not send it; and now we must be lost—*lost for ever!*

# CHAPTER XX.

## BURMAH, CHINA, ETC., ETC.

My dear children—If you will look on your map of Asia, you will see, adjoining Hindostan, at the east, a country called Burmah. This is another land of idols. Here the "Baptist General Convention for Foreign Missions" have one of the most interesting and flourishing missions in the world. The people of Burmah are, if possible, still further removed from divine knowledge than the people of India. They are in reality atheists, or, in other words, people who do not believe in a creator or preserver of the world. But still they worship gods, who, they say, have become so by acts of religious merit. He whom they now worship is called Gaudama, or Boodh. He is reputed to be the son of the king of Benares, and, if their history be correct, was born six hundred years before Christ. The Boodhists are all idolaters. They have many temples erected to the honor of Boodh and his image. Before this image they present flowers, incense, rice, betel-nuts etc. Like all other idolatrous nations, the Burmese are very wicked. They do not respect their females as they should do. They treat them as an inferior order of beings. They often sell them.

A very singular custom prevails in that country. It consists in paying a kind of homage to a white elephant. This elephant is sumptuously dressed and fed. It is provided with officers, like a second sovereign, and is made to receive presents from foreign ambassadors. It is next in rank to the king, and *superior* to the queen.

Burmah is the country in which Drs. Judson and Price, and Messrs. Hough and Wade suffered so much, during the war with England several years ago. Messrs. Hough and Wade were the first to suffer. As the ships which were to make the attack upon Rangoon approached the city, they were seized and cast into prison. Their legs were bound together with ropes, and eight or ten Burmans, armed with spears and battle-axes, were placed over them, as a guard. They were afterwards put in irons. The next morning, as the fleet approached still nearer the city, orders were sent to the guard, through the grates of their prison, that the instant the shipping should fire upon the town, they were to kill them, together with the other prisoners confined with them. The guard, on receiving these orders, began to sharpen the instruments with which they intended to kill them, and moved them about their heads to show with how much skill and pleasure they would attend to their orders. Upon the floor where they intended to butcher them, a large quantity of sand was spread to receive the blood. The gloom and silence of death reigned among the prisoners; the vast ocean of eternity seemed but a step before them. At length the fleet arrived, and the firing commenced The first ball which was thrown into the town passed, with a tremendous noise, directly over their heads. This so frightened the guard, that they seemed unable to execute their murderous orders. They shrunk away into one corner of the prison, where they remained quiet, until a broadside from one of the ships made the prison shake and tremble to its very foundation. This so alarmed them, that they burst open the doors of the prison and fled. The missionaries, with the other prisoners, were then left alone. Their danger, however, was not at an end; but as God had protected them thus far, he continued to protect them until they were set at liberty, and allowed to preach the Gospel again to those perishing heathen. Drs. Judson and Price were also imprisoned, and suffered much; but they, too, were preserved and delivered. The accounts of their sufferings are so long, that I cannot now relate them all to you. You will find them in the life of Mrs. Judson.

After the war was over, the missionaries were permitted to go everywhere to proclaim the name of the Saviour; and their efforts have been very much blessed, especially among the Karens. It will be impossible for me to give you an account of their many labors, and of the many tokens which they have received of God's favor towards multitudes who have become followers of the Redeemer. Suffice it to say, that more than six thousand have been received into the Christian church. One of the native teachers not long since baptized, on one occasion, three hundred and seventy-two persons.

Adjoining Burmah, is China, a country containing more than three hundred millions of people, about twenty times as many as there are in the United States of America. It is a country filled with idols. Many of the people earn their living by making and selling these idols. There are many shops where they are sold, or repaired when they become broken or defaced.

The females in that country are in a very degraded state. They are the slaves of their husbands, and live and die in the greatest ignorance. Any attempt to raise themselves to the level of females in Christian lands, is considered as very wicked. The little female child is tortured from her birth. You have, perhaps, heard that the women of China have small feet. These are made small by a very cruel practice—by putting bandages of cloth so tightly around them, that they cannot grow. Many women have feet not larger than those of an American infant of one year old. Mr. Doty, missionary to China, says, that he was acquainted with a little girl whose mother had bound up her feet so tightly, that she cried two or three hours every day, on account of the great pain which she suffered.

With such little feet, you may well suppose that it would be very difficult for the women to walk. It is so. They limp and hobble along, just as if their feet had been cut off, and they had to walk on stumps.

The Chinese do not count their daughters among their children. Mr. Doty says, he one day asked his Chinese teacher how many children he had. He replied, that he had several. "How many of these," he then inquired, "are daughters?" "We do not count our daughters among our children," he answered. "I have three daughters, but we Chinese count our sons only as children."

When this missionary was in a Chinese village where he had never been before, a man called to see him, bringing with him two pretty little girls, neatly dressed, about six and seven years old. He said that they were his daughters and that he wished to sell them. Mr. Doty refused to buy them, as it was wicked to buy and sell children; but he told him, that if he would commit them to him, he would take them home with him, and educate them, and that they might return home after they had grown. To this proposal he would not consent but said, that if he would buy them, they should be his for ever. He could have bought them both for about twenty-six dollars.

The Chinese have many schools, but none for their daughters, as they do not teach them, to read. When they are about thirteen years old, they shut them up in what are called "women's apartments," where they remain until the time of their marriage. Then the parents sell them to those who wish to have wives for their sons. In this way, they are frequently married to persons whom they never before saw.

Many parents in China destroy their little girls soon after they are born, or while they are very small. This they frequently do by throwing them into rivers, or into the sea, after they have wrapped them up in coarse mats. There is a little Chinese girl, named Ellen, now living in Newark, New Jersey, whose father was about to kill her when she was three weeks old. An English lady heard of his intentions, and sent a person with ten dollars to see if she could not be bought. He was offered the ten dollars, but refused to take them. She sent ten dollars more. He consented to take the twenty dollars. This little girl was brought by this English lady to America, when she was about six years old. The friends who have her under their care, are educating her with the hope that she may go back to China, to tell its females of the Saviour.

Did you ever, my dear girls, think why it is that your parents love you, and educate you—why it is that they try to make you happy, instead of cramping your feet, shutting you up, and, perhaps, at last selling you? It is because they have the Bible. Then, how anxious should you be to save what money you can, to buy Bibles to send to those poor heathen.

As I am now speaking of the destruction of infants, I would observe, that this crime is common in other heathen countries. It was quite common, until lately, in the island of Tahiti, and other places in the South Pacific Ocean. When the missionaries of the London Missionary Society went there, many years ago, they found the females in a very degraded situation. Mr. Nott, one of these missionaries, declared that three out of four of the children were murdered as soon as they were born. He met a woman soon after this dreadful crime had been abolished to whom he said, "How many children have you?" "This one in my arms," was her answer. "And how many did you kill?" She replied, "Eight." Another woman, who was asked the same question, said that she had destroyed *seventeen*. Infanticide, or, in other words, the destruction of infants, says the Rev. Mr. Williams, was carried to an almost incredible extent in Tahiti, and some other islands. He writes, "During the visit of the deputation, G. Bennet, Esq., was our guest for three or four days; and on one occasion, while conversing on this subject, he expressed a wish to obtain accurate knowledge of the extent to which this cruel practice had prevailed. Three women were sitting in the room at the time, making European garments, under Mrs. Williams direction; and, after replying to Mr. Bennet's inquiries, I said, 'I have no doubt but that each of these women has destroyed some of her children.' Mr. Bennet exclaimed, 'Impossible; such motherly, respectable women could never have been guilty of so great an atrocity.' 'Well,' I added, 'we will ask them.' Addressing the first, I said to her, 'Friend, how many children have you destroyed?' She was startled at my question, and at first charged me with unkindness, in harrowing up her feelings, by bringing the destruction of her babes to her remembrance; but upon learning the object of my inquiry, she replied, with a faltering voice, 'I have destroyed *nine*.' The second, with eyes suffused with tears, said, 'I have destroyed *seven*;' and the third informed us that she had destroyed *five*. Had the missionaries gone there but a few years before, with the blessing of God, they would have prevented all this. These mothers were all Christians at the time this conversation was held."

"On another occasion," says Mr. Williams, "I was called to visit the wife of a chief in dying circumstances. She had professed Christianity for many years, had learned to read when about sixty, and was a very active teacher in our adult school. In the prospect of death, she sent a pressing request that I would visit her immediately; and on my entering her apartment she exclaimed, 'O, servant of God, come and tell me what I must do.' Perceiving that she suffered great mental distress, I inquired the cause of it, when she replied, 'I am about to die.' 'Well,' I rejoined, 'if it be so, what creates this agony of mind?' 'O, my sins, my sins,' she cried; 'I am about to die.' I then inquired what the particular sins were which so greatly distressed her, when she exclaimed, 'O, my children, my murdered children! I am about to die, and shall meet them all at the judgment-seat of Christ.' Upon this I inquired how many children she had destroyed, and to my astonishment she replied, 'I have destroyed *sixteen*, and now I am about to die.'" After this Mr. Williams tried to comfort her, by telling her that she had done this when a heathen, and during the times of ignorance, which God winked at. But she received no consolation from this thought, and exclaimed again, "O, my children, my children." He then directed her to the "faithful saying, which is worthy of all acceptation, that Jesus Christ came into the world to save sinners." This gave her a little comfort; and after visiting her frequently, and directing her to that blood which cleanseth from all sin, he succeeded, with the blessing of God, in bringing peace to her mind. She died soon after, rejoicing in the hope that her sins, though many, would be forgiven her. Well may you exclaim, my dear children,

"Holy Bible, book divine,Precious treasure, thou art mine."

Infanticide still prevails in India, but as I have given a particular description of this crime in my Sermon to Children, on the Condition of the Heathen, I will here say nothing farher on the subject.

# CHAPTER XXI.

## THE DUTY OF PRAYING AND CONTRIBUTING FOR THE SPREAD OF THE GOSPEL.

My dear children—There is another story connected with India, which I might have mentioned in my last chapter while writing about the destruction of infants. I will relate it now, in order that you may be constrained to pray more frequently for the heathen. Some time ago, the wife of a native prince had a little daughter. The father ordered it to be put to death, immediately after it was born. Had it been a son, an heir to the throne, he would have taken great care of it. A second, a third, a fourth, a fifth little daughter was born. All these were also put to death by the command of the father. When a sixth little daughter was born, the mother's heart yearned over it. "I cannot part with it," said she; "I will have it taken away and hid, so that the king may know nothing about it." This was done, but the poor mother never dared to send for her little girl. She never saw her again, but died sometime after.

Many of the little girls in India are very pretty. They have dark eyes, and sweet, expressive countenances. This little child grew to be a very beautiful girl; and when she was eleven years old, some of her relations ventured to bring her to her father. They thought that he would be struck with the sight of his sweet child, and that he would love her for the sake of her mother who had died. The little girl fell at his feet and clasped his knees, and looked up in his face and said, "My father." And what do you think that father did? Do you think that he took her up in his arms, and kissed her? No. He seized her by the hair of her head, drew his sword from his belt, and with a single blow took off her head.

Now, my dear children, do you not think that you ought to pray for the poor heathen—to pray that God will send the Gospel to them? I want to tell you of a little boy who heard me preach some time ago about the heathen. One night he said his prayers, and went to bed. After he got into bed, he said to the nurse, "I have forgotten to pray for the heathen, and I must get out of bed and pray for them." The nurse then told him that it would not be necessary for him to get up, as he could pray for them while in bed. "No," said he, "I must get out of bed and pray for them." And the dear little boy would not rest until he got out of bed and prayed for them. Now I want all of you, my dear children, every morning and evening, to kneel down and pray for the heathen, as this little boy did. And I want you to do something more. I want you always to be punctual in attending *the usual monthly concerts of prayer,* provided there are no juvenile monthly concerts to which you can go. I have long wished to see juvenile monthly concerts of prayer established. They would be very interesting if I am to judge from the account of one which I some time ago received from a friend of mine, the Rev. Mr. V——. I will give you some extracts from his letter. He writes, "According to promise, I send you an account of the first children's monthly concert, so far as I can learn, held on Long Island. As notice was not given either in the church or Sabbath-school, the attendance was smaller than it otherwise would have been. Still, about sixty interesting children attended. After a few remarks concerning the object of the meeting by the superintendent of the Sabbath-school they sung with melting eyes the hymn that describes the wretched heathen mother casting her lovely babe into the jaws of the monster of the Granges. Prayer then was made, of about two or three minutes in length. Then I gave some of the most affecting accounts of the cruelties and ignorance of the heathen, as related by the devoted Williams, that martyr missionary. Their silent attention and subdued countenances told that their hearts were with the wretched idolaters. After having thus spent about ten minutes, the children sung in a sweet manner, a hymn—a prayer for those laboring amid the heathen:"

"When worn by toil, their spirits fail,
Bid them the glorious future hail
Bid them the crown of life survey,
And onward urge their conquering way."

"After which, two resolutions were passed, unanimously, by the children. First, that they will each one attend the monthly concert of prayer regularly, when able, and bring with them all their companions whom they can persuade to come.

"Secondly, that they, with the children of the various schools of W——, will constitute—— a life member of the W—— Bible Society. Some of the smaller children had brought their little Bibles to give them to ----, that he might carry them to the poor children of the heathen. But when informed that the heathen could not understand English, they determined to raise money, and send it out to purchase Bibles for the children. This interesting meeting was closed by prayer, the doxology, and benediction."

But not only can you pray for the heathen, you can give *something* to send the Gospel to them. Do you say that you have no money to give? But cannot you earn some? Many young persons have done so. One of whom I have read, says, "Besides supporting a school in Ceylon, we are going to support five Chinese boys. I earn six cents a week for not using tea, one for not using sugar, and three for not using coffee."

Another says, "I, with three others, have been making matches to the amount of ten dollars, and should have made more, but the people are pretty well supplied. I am going to dig my father's garden, and my mother is going to give me a quarter of a dollar for digging it, which I shall give to the missionaries. I am going to do all I can, and to earn all I can, and save all that I have, to support the missionaries."

Another says, "I am going to leave off buying candy." What is that? Can little girls and boys do without sugar-candy? I am afraid that many of you, my dear children, would find it difficult to go without it. But let me quote all that this child wrote. "I am going to leave off buying candy and such little notions, unless it is necessary, and save every cent that I can get and give it to the missionaries."

Now, my dear children, I do think that if you would save some of those cents which you spend in buying candy, fire-crackers, and similar things, and buy Bibles and tracts for the poor heathen, you would do much more good with them.

I want to tell you about a little boy who belonged to one of my schools in Ceylon, who has, as I hope, gone to heaven through the means of a tract which cost only two or three cents, and which was the cause of his coming under my care. After he had attended preaching for some time, he begged me to admit him to the church. As he was quite young, not eleven years old, I was afraid to receive him. This feeling, perhaps, was wrong. He never joined the church on earth. He has, however, I hope, gone to join the church in heaven. When he was about eleven years of age, he was attacked with the cholera and died. In this country, when children are very ill, the father or mother will catch up a cocoa-nut or a few plantains, and run off to the temple, and say, "Now, Swammie, if you will cure my little boy or little girl, I will give you this cocoa-nut, or these plantains." The mother of this boy saw that he was very ill, and she told him that she wished to go to make offerings to one of her idols, in order that he might get well. But he requested her not to do so. "I do not worship idols," said he; "I worship Christ, my Saviour. If he is pleased to spare me a little longer in the world, it will be well; if not, I shall go to him." The last words he uttered were, "I am going to Christ the Lord."

Now when you think about this little boy, I want you to ask yourselves, whether it is not better to give two or three cents to try and save the soul of some poor little heathen boy or girl, than to spend them in buying candy, and other useless things.

But I must tell you about a little girl whom I saw some time ago, who refused to buy candy while there are so many heathen without the Bible. Her father is a sea-captain. Being absent from home, he sent her five dollars to buy candy, or any thing else which she wished. As this little girl had heard about the heathen, she determined to throw all her money into the missionary-box, instead of spending it for her own pleasure. The mother, on learning her intentions, asked her if she would not like to spend a part of it for candy, and similar things. She replied, that she would not, and in due time she put her five dollars into the missionary-box. Not long after this, she was attacked with a severe toothache. The mother proposed that the defective tooth should be extracted. The little creature, for she was only about eight years old, dreaded the operation, and seemed at first to be backward about having it performed. To encourage her to submit to it, her mother offered her twenty-five cents. This little girl did not then begin to reason, Now, if I can only get those twenty-five cents, I can buy a doll, or I can buy some sugar-candy; but she reasoned thus, Now, if I can get those twenty-five cents, I can go and put them into the missionary-box. So she said to her mother, I will go and have the tooth taken out. The tooth, however, ceased to ache, but still she wished to have it extracted. Her mother then interfered, and told her that, as it had ceased to ache, it might be well for her not to have it drawn until it ached again. The little girl, however, persisted, saying, that if it were not taken out, she could not get the twenty-five cents to devote to the missionary cause. She therefore went to the dentist's, submitted to the operation, received her twenty-five cents, and went and threw them into the Lord's treasury. Was not that a noble little girl? Doubtless you will all say she was.

I must tell you about a noble little boy also. Some time ago, I was preaching to the children of Canandaigua, in the western part of New York. After I had preached there, I went on to Rochester. Returning from that place, I met with a lady in the cars, who told me as follows: "After you had preached in Canandaigua," said she, "a young lady there, who had lost her mother, and who had six or seven or eight of her brothers and sisters under her care, formed them into a missionary society." Oh, I wish that all the dear children in America were formed into missionary societies. After she had done this, she asked her little brother how he was going to get money to put into the missionary-box. "By catching mice," said he. His sister gave him two or three cents for every mouse he caught. Thus it appears, that this dear little boy was going to throw all his earnings into the Lord's treasury.

But let me tell you a little more about the children to whom I before alluded. Another says, "In some of the day-schools of this city, the girls have formed sewing societies, and make pin-cushions, needle-books, emery-bags, and the like, and send the money that is raised from the sale of them to the missionaries, to be used for the heathen. There are seven Sabbath-schools in this town, and in each of them there is a missionary association; so that in all about five hundred dollars are sent from the Sabbath-schools every year."

Now, my dear girls, I want you to think of what has now been said about the formation of sewing societies; and I want you to ask your mothers whether they will not allow you to form such societies, to meet once a week, or once in two weeks, or once a month to sew, to get some money to send the Gospel to the heathen. Many societies of this kind have been formed. After I had preached to the children in one of the churches in Third-street, New York, the little girls who attend that church formed such a society. The account which I received of it is as follows. "You may remember, that in your address to our Sabbath-school, you related instances of little girls knitting, sewing, etc., to earn something for the missionary-box The examples which you related were not lost to the girls of the Sabbath-school. Immediately they began to talk about forming themselves into a sewing society, and making small articles, and giving the proceeds to the missionary society. They did not stop here, but went right to work, and soon formed their society, which they styled the Juvenile Sewing Society. They are in a very prosperous and flourishing condition at present. I know not the amount of funds they possess—they pay a cent a week into their treasury—but they have a large assortment of articles already made. I understand, also, they meet once a week to sew."

After I had preached at a place called Little Falls, New York, the girls formed a sewing society there. The following account of this society I received from one of its little members. "When you were here last fall, and told us how much good little girls had done in having sewing societies, we thought we would see if *we* could not do some good in the world, as well as they; and, since October, we have met weekly, and by holding a fair, we have succeeded in raising sixty-two dollars. We hope it will be the means of saving some poor heathen children."

Now, as I said before, I want you, my dear girls, to ask your mothers if you may not form such societies also. Will you think of it? I hope you will.

Another of the children to whom I have twice referred, says, "I can try and save their souls, if I am not there. I can work for them, and send some money to you to buy them Bibles, and I can pray for them; and if I should save some souls, O how would they thank me. But if I did not send my money, nor care any thing about them, and I should not go to heaven, and they should not, how would they rise up in judgment against me, and say, If we had had the privileges that you had, we should not be here. O, how thankful we ought to be, that we were not born in heathen lands. O, if the poor heathen could only have such privileges as we have, how thankful would they be; and if we were born in heathen lands, I have no doubt that they would come and tell us about a Saviour."

I have received many letters from children, breathing the same spirit which is manifested in the notes I have copied.

One writes, "Last winter I brought in the wood for mother, and she gave me fifty cents. I now am very glad that I have not spent it, as I can give it to you to buy tracts for the little heathen children of India."

A second writes, "The enclosed fifty cents my grandmother gave me when I was a very little boy, for sitting still one hour. Will you please to use it to furnish the Bible and missionary to the heathen."

A third writes, "I have always spent my money for candy and other trifles, but since I have heard about the darkness and misery of the heathen, I intend to save it all, and put it into the missionary-box."

A fourth writes, "The enclosed I earned by knitting. I intended to save it, till I had sufficient to carry me a short journey to see some of my friends; but when I heard you tell about the little heathen girls, I thought I would give it to you, for the poor heathen children."

A fifth writes, "I have enclosed twelve and a half cents, which my father gave me to go and see General Tom Thumb. When I heard you lecture last evening, I came home and concluded to give it to you, and let you buy Bibles for the poor heathen."

A sixth writes, "I remember, before my mother died, she used to tell me a great deal about the children of India, and now she is in heaven. I think she would like to have me give my heart to the Saviour, and go and teach those poor children. I give you some money that was given to me to see an exhibition, which I saved to give for such things, rather than go."

A seventh writes, "You told us that two cents were the means of converting a young man. I would give two cents every week, if it would convert souls to Christ."

An eighth writes, "My mother told me, some time ago, that every day I recited my lessons without missing a word, she would give me a penny; and not being desirous to spend it, I do wish you would take it—fifty cents—to the heathen. It may buy some tracts at the bazaar or market."

A ninth writes, "We feel sorry for those poor heathen children. We will try to earn some money to buy Bibles for the heathen. Father has promised us some land to work next summer, and we think we can raise something and sell it to get the money."

A tenth writes, "Since you were here last spring, I have saved what I could—one dollar—for the heathen children, and should be glad if I could do more."

An eleventh writes, "The money which you will find enclosed, I earned by working for my mother on Saturday, which I intended to keep to buy a microscope; but when I heard you preach on Sabbath, I concluded to give it to buy Bibles for the poor heathen children."

A twelfth writes, "The enclosed, five dollars, was a birthday present from my father, but I want to give it to Dr. Scudder, for the poor little boys in Ceylon."

A thirteenth writes, "Please accept my mite, by the hand of my brother. I have been keeping it for the purpose of buying a geography; but when I heard you preach yesterday, I thought I had better send it to you, for the poor heathen."

A fourteenth writes, "I would like much to become a missionary, as I am named after one; I hope I shall be one. I have been saving a dollar to buy myself some books, but concluded to give it to buy some books for the heathen."

The last two children, whose letters you have been reading, gave to the missionary cause the money which they had been earning to buy books. When you have been earning money for the express purpose of giving it to the missionary cause, then you should devote it all to that cause; but I would advise you not to do as did the two children last mentioned. Had my opinion been asked, relative to the disposal of their money, I would have recommended them to give *one-tenth,* or perhaps a little more, of the sums they had been earning, to their Saviour, and to keep the rest to buy their books. The giving of not less than one-tenth of all you earn, for charitable purposes, is the principle which I wish to have impressed fully on your minds, and I hope you will grow up under the influence of this principle, and *never, never* depart from it. But while I thus speak, you must not suppose that I wish you to confine yourselves to the giving of one-tenth, when you can give more; I hope you will not give merely this, but one-half, or more, if you can afford it. Indeed, if you do not go as missionaries to the heathen, I want you to make it your great object *to make money for Christ, and to spend it for Christ.* O, if the generation which is grown, were as anxious to make money for Christ, and to spend it for Christ, as they are to make it for themselves, and to spend it for themselves, or to hoard it up—it may be for the everlasting destruction of the souls of their heirs—there would be no complaints that money could not be had to send the Gospel to the destitute, both at home and abroad.

In my twelfth chapter, I spoke of the liberal donations which the heathen of India make for the support of their religion. In the city of Calcutta alone, it is supposed that two millions of dollars are spent every year on the festival of a single goddess—a festival which lasts only a few days. A single native has been known to give, as I before said, more than one hundred thousand dollars at one time to this festival, and afterwards thirty thousand dollars yearly. How vast, then, must be the sums which are spent upon all the different festivals of their gods. Would that we could see such liberality among Christians. Would that we could see the generality of them willing to give even one-tenth of their annual income to the Lord. Alas, what would the heathen say, if they were to learn how much greater are the sums of money which they give to their idols, than Christians give to honor their Saviour? Would they not exclaim, It is because Christianity is false, and heathenism is true, that Christians give so little for Christ, while we give so much for our gods? My dear children, I hope that you will never allow the heathen to say that the Christian religion is false, because you do not give your money for the spread of the Gospel. Will you not resolve now, that you will, so long as God prospers you in worldly goods, give *at least* one-tenth of all you earn to the Lord? Do, my dear children, do make the resolution now.

# CHAPTER XXII.

## PERSONAL LABORS AMONG THE HEATHEN.

My dear children—You have, perhaps, often seen Campbell's missionary map of the world. If not, I want you very carefully to look at it. I want you to look at the red spots on it, and think how many millions of people embrace the religion both of the Greek and Roman Catholic churches—a religion which is nothing more nor less than paganism, with a few Christian doctrines added to it. After this, I want you to look at the green spots, and think of the hundred and twenty millions of Mohammedans, who spurn the name of Jesus as a Saviour, and who have set up Mahomet as their prophet. I want you also to look at all the dark spots, where, with comparatively a few exceptions, the people are in pagan darkness, without any knowledge of God and the only Saviour of sinners Jesus Christ. And in view of all this darkness—in view of the need of more than half a million of ministers of the Gospel to preach the news of salvation to them, I want you, my dear boys, to ask yourselves whether it may not be your duty, after you grow up, to become ministers, and go and preach the Gospel to them. You know that you are bound to do all the good to others which you can; and even if you do not love the Saviour, you are not released from your obligations to do good. I would by no means have you become ministers without giving your hearts to Christ; but this you are as much bound to do, as you are bound to do all the good you can to others. If you are not Christians, I want you, through grace, to become such, and I want many of you to become ministers and missionaries. Two of my sons are now missionaries in India, and four others, I hope, are preparing to come. And why should not you also come here, or go to other heathen lands? If you can be excused from coming or going, why may not all who are now little boys also be excused? In such a case, there will be no missionaries at all. And you know that this would be very wrong. But I do not merely want many of you, my dear boys, to become missionaries, I want many of you, my dear girls, to become missionaries also. Many little girls and boys have expressed a desire to become missionaries. Several little boys who wrote to Mr. Hutchings, one of my missionary brethren, and several little boys and girls who have written to me, have said that they would like to be missionaries.

One writes, "I should like to go and be a missionary, and instruct the poor heathen children to love God."

A second says, "I have been selling matches that I made. I got five dollars—just as many dollars as I am years old. I think I shall become a missionary, and come and help you. I hope I shall see you again when I come to Ceylon. Tell the heathen children they must love God, and be good children. They must not give the children to the crocodiles, nor throw them into the water; and they must not worship wooden and brass gods. They must worship the true God, and keep his commandments."

A third says, "I like to send money to help the poor heathen to learn to read the Bible, and other good books. I think it will be pleasant to sail across the ocean, and teach them to turn from their idols. I would teach them not to lay themselves down before the car of Juggernaut, and be crushed to death; and I would teach them not to burn themselves to death on the funeral pile."

A fourth says, "I mean to save something to send to you, to help support one school. Should my life be spared, and the way be opened at some future day, I think I should be willing to leave my native home, to go to some distant land to tell the heathen of a Saviour, whom I hope I have found."

A fifth says, "If you are ever in want of money, just please to send on to me, and I will endeavor to raise all that you want. If I live to be a man, I hope be a missionary to Ceylon or China."

One little boy wrote to me as follows: "I have for a long time been saving three shillings, for the purpose of buying a little racoon, which I intended to do on Monday. On Sunday I heard you preach, and thought I would give it to you to save some poor heathen soul; and I hope you will pray for me, that I may become a minister, and go to India, and preach to the heathen."

Another writes, "This is to certify that I, Charles D.H. Frederick, pledge myself, if God spares my life, when I get to be a man, and he pardons me through Christ Jesus, I will go and preach to the heathen."

A little girl wrote me as follows: "According to my present feelings, I should like to engage in so glorious a cause," as the missionary cause, "and I hope, when I arrive at an age to be of use to God, and the poor heathen, to embrace so glorious a cause."

Another little girl writes, "I felt very bad when I heard you tell about the poor heathen who worship the idols. I could not keep from weeping, when you told us about the man who came so far to get a teacher to come and tell the Gospel to his friends, and was disappointed. I felt very bad Sunday evening; and on Monday evening I felt that the Lord had given me a new heart. I felt happy, and sang some beautiful verses that I learned in one of mother's little books. I have read the Day-springs, and thought a great deal about the heathen for two years.

"I used to think a great deal about having nice clothes, before I thought so much about the heathen. My mother told me some time ago, that she thought she would get me a white dress when I was ten years old. I am now ten years old, and this evening mother gave me two dollars to get the dress, or dispose of it in any way I thought best; and I wish you would take it to have the poor heathen taught about the Saviour. If I live, and it is the Lord's will, I hope I shall come and help you teach the poor heathen about the Saviour."

There is a little boy in the city of New York, who formerly used to tell his mother, that he meant to be a cab-driver, and all she could say to him was of no avail in making him think differently. This little boy came with his mother to hear me preach about the heathen.

After he had left the church, as he was going home, he burst into tears, and exclaimed, "Mother, I mean to be a missionary to the heathen;" and so far as I know, he has never talked about being any thing else since. And I hope that many of you will never talk about being any thing else than missionaries to the heathen.

I am acquainted with a little girl in Ohio, who has resolved to become a missionary. She is a niece of Mr. Campbell, late missionary to Africa. She was not quite four years old when I saw her. When she was eighteen months of age, she saw the picture of a heathen mother throwing her child into the mouth of a crocodile She was deeply impressed with the sight. When she was two and a half years old, she resolved to be a missionary, and follow her uncle to Africa. From this resolution she has never drawn back. When I was at her father's house, she was asked if she would not go to India. She replied, that she would not go to India, but to Africa. She was asked why she wished to go to Africa. "To teach the heathen," was her answer. "Why should you teach the heathen?" "Because they worship idols." Her mother told me, that ever since she began to get money, she has contributed to the missionary cause; and this money has generally, if not always, been earned by some act of self-denial on her part. I hope that many of you will feel just as this little girl felt, and do just as she did.

When I was in America, I used continually, when preaching, to ask the dear children whether they would not become missionaries. I used also to beg them to write down what I had asked them. Many complied with my request. While I was at the Avon Springs, one of the daughters of a physician there, not only wrote it down, but gave me what she had written. The following is a copy of what she wrote,

*August 18, 1844.*

*Dr. Scudder requested me to come to India to help him when I am grown.*

*J. P. J.*

*Avon Springs.*

Could I raise my voice loud enough to reach America, I would beg of *you* to write down the following sentence: Dr. Scudder asks me, to-day, whether I will not hereafter become a missionary to the heathen. Perhaps you will write it down *immediately*.

Now, my dear boys, if you will come out to India, or go to Burmah or China, to tell the heathen of the Saviour, you may, with the blessing of God, do as much good as Swartz and Carey, and others have done. And if you, my dear girls, will do the same, you also may do much good. This will appear from what I am going to tell you about a little girl in Ceylon. This little girl belonged to the boarding-school at Oodooville. She early gave her heart to the Saviour, and joined the church when she was thirteen years old. I should like to know if there are any of you who have not followed her example. If so, this is not right. My dear children, it is not right. Shall this little girl, in a heathen land, a land filled with idols, give her heart to Christ; and you, in a Christian land, a land of Sabbaths, and Sabbath-schools, and Bibles, not give your hearts to him? This is not right. You know that it is not right.

But let me go on with my account of the little girl. After she had joined the church, she wanted to go and see her mother, who was a heathen, for the purpose of conversing with her about her soul's concerns. Now, in this country, when children who have been absent from their parents for any length of time go home, the mother spreads a mat down on the floor, and tells them to sit down upon it, adding that she will go and cook rice for them. They have no seats to sit on, as you have in America. Well, this little girl went home. When her mother saw her, she was very glad; and after she had spread a mat for her, and told her to sit down, she said that she would go and cook rice for her. The little girl told her that she was not hungry, and did not wish to eat, but wanted to talk with her. "You cannot talk with me," said her mother, "until I have cooked rice for you." "Mother," said the little girl, "you worship idols, and I am afraid that you will lose your soul, and I want to talk with you about Jesus Christ." The mother became quite angry with her, and rebuked her. But still the little girl continued to talk with her about her soul. The mother then became so angry, that she told her to be silent, or she would punish her. The little girl replied, "Mother, though you do whip me, I must talk to you about Jesus Christ," and she burst into tears. The mother's heart was broken. She sat down on the mat, and her little daughter talked with her, and prayed with her. After this the little girl was so troubled, fearing that her mother's soul might be lost, that she was heard praying for her during all parts of the night. And God heard her prayers. Her mother forsook her idols, and became a Christian, and her conversion was followed by the conversion of one or two others. Now, my dear little girls, if you will give your hearts to the Saviour, and in due time come here, or go to other heathen lands, and tell the people of a Saviour, you may, with the help of the Holy Spirit, be as useful as this little girl was.

Female missionaries have done much good among the heathen. I mentioned an instance on page 88, to prove this. Let me mention another instance more.

In the year 1838, an English lady, Miss Aldersey, went to the East, at her own expense to promote female education among the Chinese. At that time, she could not go to China, as that country was not open to missionaries She therefore went to Java, where there was a colony of Chinese. Here she hired a house, and collected about twenty-five girls, whom she clothed, and boarded, and taught. The Lord blessed her labors, and several of these girls were hopefully converted. When their parents saw that they would no longer worship idols, they became much opposed to the school, and some of them took their daughters from it. In the year 1842, God opened the door for the entrance of the Gospel into China. This missionary then broke up her school in Java, went to that country, and resided in the city of Ningpo. Of the girls who had become Christians while under her care, two were much persecuted by their parents. They were whipped and beaten, with the hope that they would again return to their idols; but all the efforts which were made to induce them to forsake the Saviour were in vain. They declared that they would sooner die than forsake him. When their parents saw that stripes and blows were of no avail, they determined to marry them to men who were much devoted to their idols. This stratagem, they thought, might succeed in destroying all their interest in their new religion. Here, however, they were again foiled. The girls became alarmed, and fled from their parents.

An English gentleman, but who was not a professor of religion, felt deeply interested for them, and assisted them to get on board a ship going to Batavia. Here they were pursued but escaped from the pursuers by going on board of a ship which sailed for Singapore. From Singapore they sailed for China, where they were permitted to join the old friend who had been the means of their conversion. This lady collected a school at Ningpo of more than thirty girls. Thus you see how much good female missionaries have done by going to heathen lands. And are none of you willing to follow their example? Are none of you willing to say, Here am I, Lord, send me?

# CHAPTER XXIII.

## SUCCESS OF THE GOSPEL IN INDIA AND CEYLON.

My dear Children—I have told you that India is a very dark land, but there are a few bright spots in it. Through the blessing of God upon the prayers of his people in Christian lands, and upon the prayers and labors of his missionary servants, many of the heathen of India and Ceylon have forsaken their idols, and are now enlisted under the banner of Jehovah Jesus. In the Travancore and Tinnivelly districts to say nothing of the success of the Gospel in other places, thousands and tens of thousands of the people have embraced Christianity. In hundreds of villages where but a few years ago the name of Jesus had never been heard, it is now known and adored.

You have often heard of Ceylon. If you will look at the map of Hindostan, you will find it close to that country. Here Christianity has begun to prevail. This island is two hundred miles long, and in some places quite wide. A large part of it is covered with what is called jungle. Jungle and wilderness mean the same thing. In this jungle there are many wild beasts, such as elephants, bears, wild hogs, and buffaloes. In it also, there are men, women, and children, running wild, just like the wild beasts. This people are called Verders, or wild people. They wear scarcely any clothing. They have no houses. When it rains, they creep into holes, or go under overhanging rocks. Their beds consist of a few leaves. Sunk almost to the level of the brute, they live and die like their shaggy companions of the forest. Even upon these the Gospel has tried its power. More than fifty families have settled down, forming two pleasant, and now Christian villages. They have schoolmasters and Christian teachers.

I must give you a description of two revivals of religion which occurred while I was in the island of Ceylon, in the year 1833. Before those revivals took place, there was no particular manifestation of much seriousness at any of our stations. It was in the month of October of that year, that we began to feel that we must labor more, and pray more for the conversion of perishing souls. A protracted meeting was spoken of, and it was determined that one should be held at our seminary in Batticotta—a seminary which was established for the purpose of raising up a native ministry. On the morning of the day in which the meeting was commenced, Mr. Spaulding and myself went to that station to assist Mr. Poor, the principal of the seminary, in laboring with the students. In these labors we spent five days. It was good to be there. No sooner had we begun our exercises, than a blessing from on high was experienced. The windows of heaven were opened, and the Holy Ghost descended. This was evident from the spirit of prayer which was poured out upon the pious students of the seminary. They were heard "a great while before day" pleading, in their social circles, that God would have mercy upon their impenitent companions, and bring them into the kingdom of his grace. We trust, also, that a spirit of prayer was given to those of us who took a prominent part in the meeting. At the termination of our exercises, with the exception of a few lads belonging to a Tamul class, who had lately been admitted to the seminary, there was not, so far as I know, an individual connected with it, who was not humbled at the foot of the cross, either to lie there until healed of his wounds, or to show, if he perished, that he must perish under circumstances of a very aggravated nature.

After we had finished our meeting at Batticotta we went to the female seminary at Oodooville, to hold similar meetings. Before we reached that station, the church-members there, after having heard what God was doing at Batticotta, became very much aroused to pray for the influences of the Holy Spirit to descend upon the impenitent in their seminary also. Soon after we reached the station, we held a meeting with the girls. Some of them were then deeply concerned for the salvation of their souls; but it was not until Wednesday afternoon, that we knew how powerfully the Spirit of God had been at work. The meeting which we held with the seminarists at that time was one of the most solemn meetings which I ever attended. One of them, a girl of high caste, and of a very good family, said to her companions in that meeting, "My sisters, I have been a proud one among you. I hope that if you ever see me proud again, you will tell me of it. I used to tell the missionaries, that I had given myself to the Saviour, but I had not done it." Another of the girls burst into tears, and cried out aloud. As she could not restrain her feelings, and did not wish to disturb the assembly, she arose and left it. She retired to one of the prayer-rooms adjoining the seminary, there to weep alone. She, however, was not left alone. Mr. Poor, one of my missionary associates, followed her, and endeavored to administer the consolations of the Gospel to her; but she refused to be comforted. All her distress seemed to arise from a single source. "I told you a falsehood," said she, "last Monday, in saying that I had dedicated myself to the Saviour, when I had not." Perhaps she thought at that time, that she had thus dedicated herself to the Saviour, but afterwards found that she had deceived herself. In this wretched state of mind, she continued until half-past ten o'clock that night, when she came into Mr. Spaulding's house, where I then was, and wished to know what she must do to be saved. She was told, as she had often been told before, that she must dedicate herself entirely to her Saviour. She went away, and returned the same night at about half-past eleven o'clock, saying, that she had found HIM.

"Friends, is not my case amazing? What a Saviour I have found."

My dear young friends, are there any of you who have never given your hearts to Christ? If so, let me entreat you to follow the example of that dear little girl of whom I have now been speaking. She found it to be necessary to give her heart to the Saviour, and I hope that she did give it to him. O that you too might give up your hearts to him. Alas, if you do not, you must soon go down to eternal burnings where you will be constrained to cry out, Lost, lost, lost for ever! Be careful, my dear children, O be careful that this young girl does not rise up against you in the last day, and condemn you. She must do so—she will do so, if you do not, like her, choose Christ as your portion. But I am digressing, and must go back to the point I left.

The next day, one of our missionary sisters, who had lately reached Ceylon from America, came to Oodooville, to witness the nature of the work which she heard was in progress at that place. As she was entering Mr. Spaulding's house, she was met by one of the most consistent church-members of the seminary, who declared that she had lost her hope of being a Christian. Perhaps this church-member was disposed to write bitter things against herself because she did not feel all that warmth in religion which marked the conduct of those who, at that time, were indulging the hope that they had passed from death to life. After the sister to whom I alluded had been in the house a little while, she requested Mrs. Spaulding to allow her to have an interview with such of the girls as were entertaining a hope of their interest in the Saviour. These were twenty-two in number. This interview was granted. As she knew nothing about the Tamul language, I acted as her interpreter. Through me, she requested the girls to give a statement of their feelings. One of them arose, and said, "I feel as happy as an angel. I feel joys that I can express to no one but my Saviour; and I am just as certain that my sins are forgiven, as if I had sent up a karduthaase," that is, a letter to heaven, "and received an answer to it." Another of the girls said, that the missionaries had often talked with her about her dedicating herself to the Saviour, but that she did not then know what it meant. "I now know," added she, "what it means, for God has taught it to me." Another of the girls said, "Though they put me in the fire, I will never forsake the Saviour."

Now, my dear children, I must bid you farewell Probably I shall never see you, unless you come to this heathen land, until I meet you at the judgment-seat of Christ. If you do not become missionaries, most of you will probably die, and be buried where you now are. Probably I shall die in this heathen land. But we shall not always sleep in our graves. After a little season, the archangel's trumpet will sound, and you in America, and I in India, shall hear his voice proclaiming, "Awake, ye dead, and come to judgment." And we shall all at once rise from our graves, and stand before our Judge. And where shall I then see you? Shall I see any of you on the left hand of Christ, and hear him say, "Depart, ye cursed, into everlasting fire, prepared for the devil and his angels?" O, if I should hear that dreadful sentence pronounced against you, how would my heart die within me. How could I bear to hear it. Oh, I could not—I could not bear to hear it. My dear children, if you are yet out of Christ, I entreat you, *at this very moment*, to lay down this book, and throw yourselves at the feet of your Saviour. Tell him, that you are lost sinners, deserving to be cast into everlasting burnings. Tell him, that though you have been wicked children, you will leave off your wickedness, and be his for ever. Plead with him, with as much earnestness as a *drowning* man would plead with you to save him, to give you the influences of his Holy Spirit, to create within you a clean heart, and renew within you a right spirit, without which you are eternally undone; and continue to plead, until he pardons you, and receives you as his children. By all the sufferings of the Son of God, by all the joys of heaven, by all the torments of hell, by the solemnities of your dying bed, by the value of your immortal souls *which, if once lost, must be lost for ever*, I beseech you thus *immediately* to throw yourselves at his feet, and plead with him to make you his. Neglect this duty—neglect giving yourselves to Christ, even for one minute, and it may be, that you will be lost, yea, LOST FOR EVER.

Milton Keynes UK
Ingram Content Group UK Ltd.
UKHW040901050124
435493UK00006B/988